Bibliographic information published by the German National Library:

The German National Library lists this publication in the National Bibliography;
detailed bibliographic data are available on the Internet at http://dnb.dnb.de .

Imprint:

Copyright © 2015 GRIN Verlag, Open Publishing GmbH
Print and binding: Books on Demand GmbH, Norderstedt Germany
ISBN: 978-3-668-06942-8

This book at GRIN:

http://www.grin.com/en/e-book/308306/nfc-based-platforms-in-gaming-reverse-
engineering-nintendos-amiibo

Thomas Petereder

NFC based platforms in gaming. Reverse engineering Nintendos "Amiibo"

GRIN Publishing

GRIN - Your knowledge has value

Since its foundation in 1998, GRIN has specialized in publishing academic texts by students, college teachers and other academics as e-book and printed book. The website www.grin.com is an ideal platform for presenting term papers, final papers, scientific essays, dissertations and specialist books.

Visit us on the internet:

http://www.grin.com/

http://www.facebook.com/grincom

http://www.twitter.com/grin_com

Near field communication based platforms in gaming

Thomas Petereder

BACHELORARBEIT

eingereicht am

Fachhochschul-Bachelorstudiengang

Mobile Computing

in Hagenberg

im September 2015

Contents

Preface

As a gamer I like harsh challenges: no *Super Smash Bros.* opponent can be too strong, no *Super Mario* level can be too tricky and no zombie horde can be too big. The most I thus love about these trials is the satisfying moment you get whenever the challenge is finally beaten. This bachelor thesis however has yet been my hardest quest so far. Luckily, I have had several teammates who accompanied me on this very long journey. Some of them whom I would like to thank a lot, now that this game is over.

First of all I would like to thank my brother Stefan, as without him I would probably have never started playing video games in the first place. Without this strong passion in my life I would also have never chosen the topic of "*NFC* based platforms in gaming" for my bachelor thesis.

Furthermore, I would like to thank my parents Albert and Ursula, as they constantly encouraged me to keep writing. Also I am really grateful that my close friends, Dominik and Manuel, distracted me from working on the bachelor thesis every time I already needed a break and some time off in order to play video games with them.

Moreover, I would like to thank my beloved girlfriend Melanie, as without her continual help and comfort I surely would have dropped out of university a long time ago.

And finally I would like to show a very special gratitude to my dear sister Karin, as she always contributed valuable advice, whenever I needed her help.

Abstract

Near Field Communication (*NFC*) gained more and more popularity over the past few years. As a result, the number of applications suitable for the daily usage increases continuously. With the gaming industry being one of the fastest growing markets nowadays, it was just a matter of time, until these two fields of research met.

This bachelor thesis hence gives an overview about the *near field communication* technology and further tries to enlighten the concept of *NFC*-based platforms in gaming. In order to give a concrete example for this, a technology called *Amiibo* is examined with the corresponding software project based on it.

Chapter 1

Introduction

1.1 Motivation

It feels as if it just had been yesterday that my elder brother compelled me to play a video game with him, though this happened back in 1996. The new concept of playing immediately fascinated me from the very beginning and ever since I contribute most of my leisure to the topic of video games. As an approximation I spend an average of about three to five hours per day playing games.

According to a recently published statistic of the *Entertainment Software Association*[10] at least 155 million United States citizens are keen on the exact same passion. This results in the video game industry being one of the fastest growing markets worldwide. Therefore, it is hardly surprising that every year new technologies emerge within this segment.

This bachelor thesis hence is about one of the fastest growing of these technologies, combining *near field communication (NFC)* chips with videogames.

1.2 State of the art

Near field communication has a wide variety of applications, but there is one that constantly gains more and more popularity amongst the public. It is the field of gaming, where *NFC* is nowadays frequently used.

1.2.1 Gami cation

The term *gamification* describes the utilization of mechanics, logic or rules that are common in videogames in other non-game related applications. The purpose of this is mainly to encourage the user to interact with the given system, as otherwise the initiative of one's own to do so would be nominal. *Gamification* therefore tries to make techniques or content more appealing

1

and to further prolong the overall motivation. This is enhanced due to the fact that people tend to willingly perform tasks as part of a game, even though these tasks might be considered boring otherwise.

Taken from Erik Einebrant[15], *Nokia* (a communications and information technology company from Finland) had been one of the first supporters of *NFC* and *gamification*. For this, he listed the example of *Nokia Shakespeare Shu e*. Several cards with *NFC* tags (each storing a line of a famous Shakespeare quote) must be rearranged in the correct order. To do so, a *NFC* enabled phone must be touched to one of these cards, as this causes the corresponding part of the quote to be played.

1.2.2   Mixed reality gaming

Mixed reality is an environment in between of the real and the virtual world and is hence a combination of both. Taken from Hinske et al.[19], Benford stated, that:

> *Pervasive games extend the gaming experience out into the real world. While in the game, the player becomes unchained from the console and experiences a game that is interwoven with the real world and is potentially available at any place and any time.*

Therefore, *pervasive games* (a subset of mixed reality games) are digital goods with a strong connection to the real world and therefore they create a virtual reality. As an example for this, digital interfaces can be integrated within items of everyday life in such a way that they are hardly distinguishable. Based on that fact the "toy to life"-concept emerged.

1.2.3   Toy to life -concept

In 2007 *Mattel*, an American toy manufacturing company, tried to revolutionize their sector by inventing a completely new concept for toys. For this, they launched *U.B. Funkeys*, a series of small plastic figurines containing *NFC* tags within. The main idea behind this product was that every figure could unlock certain features (mini-games, characters, designs, etc.) within an online video game, once the toys are placed on a *NFC*-reader connected to the PC. Though this concept was of great potential, the series flopped and was discontinued in early 2010. Later on other companies took up this issue and launched their own products. Therefore, at the time of writing, three big franchises (and one - *Lego Dimensions* - being in development) exist within this segment.

- *Skylanders*
  The video game publisher *Activision* learned from the mistakes of their predecessor *Mattel* and launched the *Skylanders* series. As *Mattel*

mainly focused on their product being appealing to collectors, *Activision* used their profound knowledge in the field of gaming in order to better adapt to the target group of gamers. Furthermore, *Activision* employed the former iconic *PlayStation* figure *Spyro the Dragon* to their advantage, as becoming the new official mascot for the *Skylanders* series. As of February 2015, the *Skylanders* series has sold a total number of 175 million toys since its initial launch in 2011. The *Skylanders* series is hence one of the top 20 highest-selling video game franchises of all time.

Figure 1.1: Examples of *Skylanders* figurines, adapted from http://www.cnet.com/au/products/skylanders-trap-team-starter-pack-androi d-i os/2/

In order to connect the digital and the physical world, *Activision* wrapped a unique storyline around the *Skylanders* series. For this, a villain called *Kaos* invaded the kingdom of *Skyland* and banished its inhabitants, the *Skylanders*, to the human world as toys. Thus it is the player's duty to send them back into the game and respectively to their homes. To do so, a *Skylander*-toy is placed atop the so-called *Portal of Power* (a *NFC*-reader connected to the videogame console via USB or Bluetooth) and immediately comes to life within the game. As the videogame itself takes the form of a traditional RPG (role-playing game)[13] the player is now able to control the unlocked figurine. With the proceeding progress the character gains more experience and acquires more abilities, which however are all stored on the physical game piece rather than on the gaming console. As a result, the player can use the own game characters on any other device, irrespective of the used console type, with all their attributes and skills being intact.

- *Disney Infinity*
  Thanks to the *Skylanders* series the way for a commercial application of *NFC* in gaming had been smoothed and so it was just a matter of time that *Activision* got its first competitor in 2013 with *Disney Infinity*.
  Disney Infinity is an action-adventure open-world video game (the player is given significant freedom as being able to move freely through a virtual world and to approach any objective at any time). Thus

the game has no specific storyline. However, by connecting a *Disney Infinity* figurine with the gaming console the specific character, as well as a campaign strongly connected to the corresponding franchise, will become unlocked and playable within the game. Altogether the available figures are all taken from existing *Disney* and *Pixar* licenses, and therefore the assortment is frequently extended.

Figure 1.2: Examples of *Disney Infinity* figurines, taken from http:// www.v -gamers.com/wp-content/uploads/2014/10/Di sney-Infi ni ty-2.0_Av engers_Gruppe.jpg

- *Amiibo*
  In 2014 *Nintendo* followed the trend of *Skylanders* and *Disney Infinity* with their own product line, called *Amiibo*. Until the end of 2014 approximately 5.7 million *Amiibo* toys had been sold worldwide, whereas in May 2015 already 10.5 million units had been shipped.
  The characters represented by *Amiibos* are taken from different *Nintendo* franchises. As a matter of fact and in strong comparison to the two competitors, *Amiibos* are not bound to a single game and therefore exhibit a wider variation of applications. For this, two types of video games need to be differed. The ones that only read data from the *Amiibos* and the others with saving permission as well. The first type mostly will unlock new content within a certain game, such as new skins (the character's appearance or costume), new weapons, new playable characters and so on, whereas the second type however is a bit more complex. Taking the example of the beat 'em up *Super Smash Bros.* (for *Nintendo Wii U* and *Nintendo 3DS*), with the aid of *Amiibos*, artificial intelligences (AIs) can be trained and stored on the *NFC* tag. As a result, one's play style will be copied by the figurine.

A promotion tournament hosted by *Nintendo* had shown that the AIs are even capable of defeating real players with ease, as a *Fox McCloud Amiibo* almost had won the tournament and was ranked second place.

Figure 1.3: Examples of *Amiibo* figurines, taken from http://www.i ngame.de/arti kel/ami i bo-ni ntendo-v ersteht-frustrati on-der-kunden-und-v erspri cht-nachschub/

When *Nintendo* was founded back in 1889, the company solely retailed traditional Japanese *Hanafuda* playing cards. Hence with the lately announced *Amiibo* cards they somehow try to go back to their roots. In this context *Amiibo* cards are the much cheaper versions of their figure-based counterparts bringing along the exact same functionality. However, by selling them in packs of six random cards hidden from view, the end user is further conduced to collect and to swap cards with colleagues.

Figure 1.4: Examples of *Amiibo* cards, taken from http://www.i heartami i bo.com/wp-content/uploads/2015/07/cards.jpg

Unlike their competitors in the "toy to life"-market, *Nintendo* shows to be more innovative in the variety of their product lines. Besides the profound plastic figure based *Amiibos* and the *Amiibo* cards the company started to offer a collection of *Amiibos* made of yarn. Shortly after their release almost the entire stocking of the yarn *Amiibos* had been sold and units can hardly be found in retail. Due to this rush and for the enormous fan-base, *Nintendo* revealed to even launch an oversized variation of the popular *Green Yarn Yoshi Amiibo* by the end of November 2015.

Figure 1.5: Yarn *Amiibos* from the *Yoshi's Woolly World* collection, taken from http://www.polygon.com/2015/8/24/9200829/yam-yoshi -ami i bo-mega-release-date-pri ce

Due to this bachelor thesis, as well as the corresponding software project being based on *Amiibos*, this technology and its functionality is described in more detail later on in chapter 3.

- *Lego Dimensions*
  Besides the well-established product line of plastic construction toys, *Lego* branched out into the video gaming market since 1997. The enormous variety of cooperating partners enabled *Lego* to exhibit thousands of sets based upon all different kinds of franchises (like *Star Wars, Jurassic Park, Batman*, etc.). Hence this product diversity directly reflects to their gaming segment as well and furthermore plays an important role within the upcoming (release date is set to September 2015) "toy to life"-video game of *Lego Dimensions*. For this, *Lego Dimensions* follows the same format as *Skylanders, Disney Infinity* or as the *Amiibo* series, but with *NFC*-enabled *Lego* figurines that will, once scanned, unlock new content (level, vehicles, playable characters, etc.) within the game. As it is typical for *Lego*, these figures are sold as a set of several pieces which need to be connected first, in order to finally build the proper construct.

Figure 1.6: Examples of *Lego Dimensions, taken from http://www.toysrus.com/graphics/tru_prod_images/LEGO-Dimensions-Fun-Pack--Emmet--pTRU1-21175848dt.jpg*

- **Amiibo-Skylander** crossover

  The *Electronic Entertainment Expo* (commonly known as E^3) as the world's biggest annual exhibition for video games is generally used to announce upcoming video game product lines, consoles and games per se. Due to the tremendous and overall increasing demand for *Skylanders* as well as for *Amiibos*, *Activision* and *Nintendo* joined forces and revealed at 2015's E^3 that both will launch *Amiibo-Skylander* figures in a special crossover line-up. For this, *Activision* made the first move by introducing their latest *Skylanders* installment of *Skylanders: Super Chargers*, which is going to be released in September 2015.

  Special about this product line is that a total amount of two *near field communication* tags is integrated within each figure. By twisting the bottom plate the figurines can either individually function as an *Amiibo* or as a *Skylander*.

Figure 1.7: Examples of the *Amiibo-Skylander* crossover line-up, taken from http://www.toysrus.com/graphi cs/tru_prod_i mages/LEGO-Di mensi ons-Fun-Pack--Emmet--pTRU1-21175848dt.jpg

- **Pokémon Rumble**

  Already one year before the initial rollout of *Amiibos*, *Nintendo* launched their product line of *Pokémon Rumble NFC* figurines. As this happened slightly before *Disney Infinity* emerged, the "toy to life"-concept was still a niche market back then. Therefore, and due to a lack of usages for these figures (by scanning, the *Pokémon* depicted by the figurine could be used in-game) in solely one mediocre game called *Pokémon Rumble U*, this technology never lived up to its expectations. Nevertheless a total amount of 24 different figures had been launched. As it is typical for the *Pokémon* franchise, the so-called *pocket monsters* are stored in separate capsules, the well-known *PokéBalls*. This is another marketing strategy, as the customer never knows which figure will be received within the next purchase. The *Pokémon* fan base however is quite familiar with this concept, as within the *Pokémon* series, the gamers are also animated to swap their beloved *Pokémon* with each other. As a result this technology was not entirely considered to be a flop, as at least the dedicated fan base pulled in sales. The *Pokémon Rumble* figures are, at the time of writing, not yet completely discontinued, whereas some units might still be sporadically found in retail. This is assumed to be a direct consequence of the market entrance of *Amiibos*, as *Nintendo* clearly revisited this concept with the latter.

Figure 1.8: Examples of some *Pokémon Rumble NFC* figures, taken from http://www.ami i botoys.com/wp-content/uploads/2014/10/pokemonami i bo.jpg

Chapter 2

Near field communication

Near field communication (*NFC*) is basically a short-range wireless connection between two nodes used for information transfer. This technology is further based on the already existing and profound method of *Radio Frequency Identification* (abbreviated by *RFID*). Langer and Roland state in their publication that the first usage of *RFID* dates all the way back to the *Second World War*[24].

2.1 *Radio frequency identification* (*RFID*)

Radio frequency identification is a system for the contactless identification and data-transfer throughout electromagnetic waves. For this purpose tags (transponders for emitting messages) and corresponding readers are required.

In most cases a *RFID* tag contains an identification number, by which the *RFID* reader can identify the read object. Furthermore, tags might also store read- and/or writable memory within.

Depending on their electric power source, *RFID* tags can be generally divided into two groups.

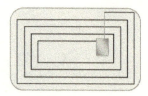

Figure 2.1: Scheme of a *RFID* tag including chip and coil[14]

9

2.1.1   Active *RFID*

Active tags have their own power source and hence they can transmit a stronger signal over a further distance (up to 20 or 100 meter). In exchange for these features the tag however is bigger and more expensive than their passive counterparts. For active tags it is either possible to constantly broadcast a signal, or to stay dormant until a receiver comes within range. Due to having their own on-board power source, active tags typically operate at higher frequencies of about 2.45 - 5.8GHz, depending on the use case and memory requirements.

2.1.2   Passive *RFID*

On the other hand passive *RFID* tags do not possess their own power source, so these tags are rather cheap in production (according to Weinstein less than $0.2 per piece[32]) and as a result established as a standard in *RFID* implementations. In addition passive tags are rather small, compared to the active ones. As for the signaling distance, there is a very general rule of thumb: *The larger the tag, the larger the read range.* [32]

2.2   *Near field communication* (*NFC*)

2.2.1   Evolution of *NFC*

According to Langer and Roland[24], the *NFC* technology had been invented by *Sony* and *NXP Semiconductors* (former *Philips Semiconductors*) back in 2002. Later on in 2004, the *NFC Forum* was founded by the former and *Nokia* with the purpose to uniformly standardize the *NFC* technology worldwide. At that time, *Nokia* had been one of the biggest and well established manufacturers for mobile-phones, and therefore, with the implementation within several of their devices, *near field communication* started its triumph. Ever since, many field trials had been launched worldwide in order to exhibit and test new fields of application. By way of example, Langer and Roland refer to the field trial in the *University of applied Sciences Hagenberg* in 2006. For this, the participants (mostly students and teachers) were, under the usage of *NFC*-enabled phones, able to purchase meals in two canteens on the one hand, and on the other the subscribers could gain access to lecture halls and laboratories.

Over the long term many applications for *NFC* in everyday life could be established. The most common for this are service initiation (*NFC* tags are located within ordinary items and by connecting a corresponding reader bits of information about the given object can easily be obtained), peer-to-peer connections, mobile *NFC* payment and, as already listed in the first chapter, small plastic figurines used for gaming.

2.2.2 Functional principle

2.2.2.1 Power supply

The *near field communication* technology is based on *radio frequency identification* and hence *NFC* tags also either possess an active or a passive power supply.

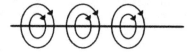

Figure 2.2: Magnetic field of a current-carrying conductor[24]

Hans Christian Ørsted had proven in 1820 that every current-carrying conductor produces a magnetic field(figure 2.2). As coils are numerously curled conductors, the generated magnetic field hence is heavily amplified within. Contradictorily, in case a particle of charge enters an electromagnetic field, it will experience a force orthogonal to the direction of the magnetism and electricity - the so-called *Lorentz force*. Michael Faraday postulated that vice versa changes in the magnetic field might affect the electrons to flow within a conductor, as the raised *Lorentz force* drives them within a certain direction. The therefore generated power is known to us as induced current. One use of the induced current that is essential for passive *RFID* (and respectively for passive *NFC*) are transformers. For this, one coil running on alternating current is located right next to another coil. Due to the constant flux alteration, potential is inducted within the second choke. The gained voltage is direct proportion to the coils' windings ($U_1 : U_2 = N_1 : N_2$).

The basic structure of a *RFID* or *NFC* system using induction is displayed in figure 2.3. For the power allocation the reader feeds its antenna (coil 1) with a sinusoidal current and as a matter of fact the transponder antenna therefore receives inducted electricity. In order to access the received alternating current as a direct one, a rectifier is then used. As due to slight changes in the inductive coupling (distance between reader and transponder increases/decreases or the transponder gets repositioned) the received inducted current, within the transponder, changes enormously. But the tags and their integrated circuits mostly operate only within a smaller voltage range (currently from approximately 0.8 to 5 volt). Thus a voltage limiter is required in order to either amplify or limit the voltage.

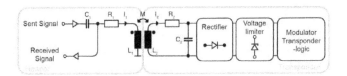

Figure 2.3: Structure of a *RFID/NFC* system using induction[24]

2.2.2.2 Data transfer

Depending on the power supply (active or passive) there are two kinds of data transmission for *RFID*- and *NFC*-systems. For passive systems, the tags' roles (one is the reader and the other one is the transmitter) are fixed and hence two channels are used. Whereas for active systems, the currently transmitting device always acts as the reading and writing unit, but the roles are not predefined whereby these can be switched. In this case, only one channel is used for the data transfer. But in comparison to *RFID*, *NFC* always operates on the frequency band of 13.56MHz.

The uplink (transfer from reader to the transponder) is equal to the direction of the power supply. Therefore, it seems obvious to modulate the carrier signal which is used for supplying the energy with the data stream. Most commonly *amplitude-shift-keying* and *phase-shift-keying* are used for this.

Then again the downlink is the transponder's response passed on to the reader generated by load modulation. Changes in the transponder's impedance result in a different amplitude or even phase of the potential at the receiving antenna which will then get demodulated as the responded signal. In order to simplify, one could assume that the receiving tag alters the magnetic field generated by the reader, as it uses up energy. As a matter of fact less power is retransmitted and, due to this deviation, the reader is hence capable of reconstructing the received data. In *RFID*- and *NFC*-systems there are two possible types of load modulation. For one thing ohmic load modulation, whereas for another thing capacitive load modulation exists. The former causes merely *ASK* (*amplitude-shift-keying*) for the receiving antenna's voltage, as an additional modulation resistor is wired parallel to the transponder's own transistor. The latter in comparison however induces *ASK* as well as *PSK* (*phase-shift-keying*) on the retransmitting potential, as an additional modulation capacitor is wired parallel to the transponder's own condenser.

2.2.2.3 Anti-collision

As simultaneously more than one tag can be in the *RFID/NFC*-reader's range, and furthermore all of them even transmit on the same frequency band, the sent data streams interfere and are hence damaged by collisions. To avoid this behavior multiplexing is applied. Due to the fact that only one frequency band is utilized, *FDMA* (*frequency-division multiple access*) cannot be used. *CDMA* (*code-division multiple access*) is not suitable either, as the upcoming streams are transmitted at staggered intervals, due to the various distances between tag and reader. Consequently, *TDMA* (*time-division multiplexing*) and *SDMA* (*space-division multiplexing*) are commonly available for *RFID*- and *NFC*-systems. In addition to these procedures, several anti-collision methods can be used for increased reliability.

- **Collision avoidance**
  One of the easiest, but not less target-aimed, models for this purpose is the concept of collision avoidance. For this, every communication node checks beforehand if no other communication has yet been established. Taking the example of a *NFC*-based system, a node only activates its own carrier signal once no other radio frequency field has been detected over a certain, but randomly chosen, timespan.

- **Binary search**
  On the other hand, *NFC*-systems can benefit from using a binary search algorithm to detect every transponder within reach. As every tag has its own identification, the reader first gathers every one of these. In case the reader receives multiple IDs a collision is detected. Therefore, the reader starts a recursion in order to ask for the first half of the obtained identifiers. This is performed several times while the reader receives more than one ID at a time. Assuming that only one value is returned however, the reader can now access the corresponding transponder throughout the newly received identifier. Whereas if nothing is returned, the reader will start another recursion for the second half of the ID-array. Throughout the entire search process all tags will get enumerated.

- **Slotted *ALOHA***
  At first sight the *ALOHA* protocol seems to be the complete opposite of collision avoidance. Whenever a communication node has data to send, the information will be transmitted at a randomly chosen point. Taking the case that by hazard more than one node simultaneously broadcast their data, a collision is detected. In this scenario every communication participant will be requested to try to resend the collided data packages

after a short, but yet once again, randomly chosen timespan. As it is most likely that the repeated data streams will interfere again after the aforesaid intermission, discrete timeslots were introduced in the improved slotted *ALOHA* protocol. For this, the receiver forwards further details about the duration of the pausing process (in multiples of timeslots) as an extra parameter to the communication nodes, alongside the query for resending collided data. Therefore, with the usage of timeslots, the collisions are overall reduced and hence as a result the maximum throughput is increased significantly.

2.2.2.4 Signaling technologies

For *NFC* devices three signaling technologies exist, in order to ensure that various types of *near field communication* can communicate with each other. Whenever a tag comes within a reader's range, they first communicate about the used technology and transmit data based on the specified protocols[1].

- **NFC-A** (*ISO/IEC 14443 Type A*)
  As the name already implies, *NFC-A* only corresponds with the compatible *RFID Type A* communication. In *Type A* communication delay encoding (*Miller encoding*) is used. For this set-up a sent signal needs to change from 0 to 100 percent, in order for the device to register the difference between sending a 1_2 or a 0_2 bit. Data rates of approximately $106Kb/s$ can be achieved by using this signaling technology[1].

- **NFC-B** (*ISO/IEC 14443 Type B*)
  Similar to *NFC-A*, *NFC-B* solely corresponds with *RFID Type B* communication. However, a *Type B* communication uses *Manchester encoding*, instead of *Miller encoding* utilized by the *NFC-A* counterpart. By any definition, the amplitude modulation is at 10 percent, resulting in a falling edge (from 100% to 90%) being represented by a logic 1_2, whereas a rising edge (from 90% to 100%) is resembled by a logic 0_2[1].

- **NFC-F** (*JIS X 6319-4 - FeliCa*)
  In strong comparison to the other two signaling technologies, this one however is normalized by the *Japanese Industrial Standards Committee*. *NFC-F* further refers to a faster form of *RFID* transmission (data rates with up to $212Kb/s$) known as *FeliCa*[24].

2.2.2.5 Communication modes

For *NFC*-devices it is possible to operate within three standardized communication schemes: *Peer-to-Peer, Reader/Writer Mode & Card Emulation*[2].

- **Peer-to-Peer Mode**
  Two *NFC* enabled devices can communicate with each other, in order to exchange information or to share files, while they both operate in *Peer-to-Peer Mode*. For this, at least one partner uses active *NFC* and both make use of the *Logical Link Control Protocol (LLCP)*; a protocol that supports the bi-directional communication.

- **Reader/Writer Mode**
  The *Reader/Writer Mode* enables the communication between an active *NFC*-device and a passive tag, whereas data can be read from or written to the tag. In order to grant a successful transmission, the used data format needs to come up to the standard of the *NFC Data Exchange Format*, as it will be described later on(see 2.2.3).

- **Card Emulation Mode**
  In the *Card Emulation Mode* a *NFC* enabled device can act as, and therefore tries to emulate, a *NFC* tag. Instead of the bi-directional communication used in *Peer-to-Peer Mode*, a direct one (only the reader gets bits of information stored on the virtual *NFC* tag) is established, as the emulated tag uses passive *NFC*.

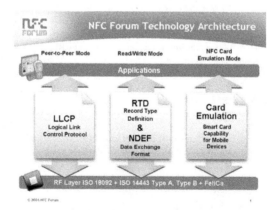

Figure 2.4: *NFC*-communication modes[14]

2.2.3   NFC Data Exchange Format (NDEF)

The *NFC Data Exchange Format* specification defines the format, as well as the rules, of the required data structure that is used in order to exchange bits of information between two *NFC* enabled devices or a *NFC*-reader and the corresponding tag. Therefore, *NDEF* is a simple binary data-format containing application-specific data. The application-specific data, as well as meta information (information about the possible interpretation, the structure of one *NDEF Record*, etc.) are packed into so-called *NDEF Records*. Then again several *NDEF Records* might be grouped as a *NDEF Message*. As an example take the case of two *NFC*-devices sharing contact information with each other. The entire contact is therefore submitted as one *NDEF Message* containing several *NDEF Records* (the contact's name/phone number/etc.). Hence based upon different underlying transfer protocols (e.g. *Logical Link Control Protocol* (*LLCP*)) a unified format for the data transmission is granted[24].

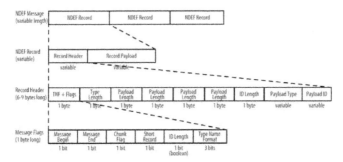

Figure 2.5: *NDEF Message* structure[5]

2.2.3.1   NDEF Record

As already mentioned before, a *NDEF Record* consists out of meta information, as well as the actual application-specific data. Respectively the *NDEF Record* is subdivided into a header (the meta information) and a payload (the data). Moreover the header has *Boolean* flags, length specifications of certain fields (**Type Length, Payload Length & ID Length**), information about the used data type (*TNF* (*type name format*) & **Payload Type**) and optionally a unique identifier for the data packet stored within (**Payload ID**). The flags in questions are further categorized as: **MB**

(**Message Begin**), **ME** (**Message End**), **CF** (**Chunk Flag**), **SR** (**Short Record**) and **IL** (**ID Length Present**). **MB** and **ME** typically mark the first and last *NDEF Record* within the entire *NDEF Message*, whereas **CF** indicates whether this entry is complete or separated and continued within (at least) the following *NDEF Record*. **SR** on the other hand signalizes a shorter *NDEF Record*, as the payload's length is reduced from 32 bits (flag set to 0_2) to 8 bits (flag set to 1_2). Finally the value of the **IL** flag resembles the state of the *NDEF Record*'s identification information. In case this flag is not set to *true*, the record does neither contain the **ID Length** nor the ID field. Otherwise an **ID Length** value is set which moreover defines the bit length of the ID Field per se.

2.2.3.2 *NDEF Message*

A *NDEF Message* contains at least one *NDEF Record*, but in most cases several entries are grouped within. Throughout bits in the single *NDEF Records'* headers the beginning and the end of the messages are marked (with flags for **Message Begin** & **Message End**).

2.2.3.3 *NFC Record Type Definition (RTD)*

With *NDEF Messages* and the underlying protocols all different kinds of data formats can be transmitted. However, no bits of information about how the *NFC* enabled device should interpret and handle the newly received data are given. Therefore, the *NFC Record Type Definition* clearly defines basic structures and guidelines for the further proceeding and representation of the data on the *NFC* device. For this, *RTD* has on the one hand a basic specification, mostly in order to handle essential parameters, such as naming conventions, the proceeding of defective or unknown *RTD*s, as well as rules for the conjunction of several *NDEF Records* and *NDEF Messages*. On the other hand *RTD* has further specifications regarding the different record types as these are already declared in the *NDEF Records*' **TNF**s and **Payload Type** fields. On the basis of the **TNF** exactly two types of *NDEF Records* can be defined and thus are marked by *Uniform Resource Names* (*URN*)[24]:

- *NFC Forum Well-known Types*
  NFC Forum Well-known Types are reserved by the *NFC Forum* and fit the scheme urn:nfc:wkt:<Name>. In order to keep the used memory consumption low, solely the *URN* <Name> is saved within the *NDEF Record*'s type field. Basically there is a separation between global and local types. The global types are declared and predefined by the *NFC Forum* and hence must not hardly differ from the pristine *RTD*-definition, whereas the local types can be freely defined within the

context of one actual field of application. The most common examples for *NFC Forum Well-known Types* are: *Text Record types (wkt : T)*, *URI Record types (wkt : U)*, *Smart Poster Record types (wkt : Sp)*, *Generic Control Record types (wkt : Gc)* & *Signature Record types (wkt : Sig)*.

- **NFC Forum External Types**
  By contrast *NFC Forum External Types* must not fit the specifications through the *NFC Forum* at all, whereas organizations can define their own arbitrary record types. In order to distinguish between *Well-known Types* and *External Types*, urn:nfc:ext:<Domain>:<Name> is used as the *URN* pattern for the latter ones. Like for the *NFC Forum Well-known* counterparts, only the *URN* <Domain>:<Name> is saved within the *NDEF Record*.

Chapter 3

Reverse engineering *Amiibo*

For the *University of Applied Sciences Hagenberg*, especially for the bachelor
degree course *Mobile Computing*, it is most common to submit a software
project alongside the bachelor thesis. At first an *Android* library for the
basic *Amiibo* integration, as well as an *Android* application for the emulation of *Amiibos*, had been targeted. But several difficulties arose within the
development phase, whereas the scope of the software project was changed
to the *Android* library in question and an *Android* application in order to
backup *Amiibo* data.

Hence within the following chapter *Amiibos* and their functionality, the
research results of analyzing *Amiibos*, the development phase and the difficulties within and last, but not least, the software project per se will be
described in more detail.

3.1 *NFC* tag

The *International Organization for Standardization* (*ISO*), as well as the
NFC Forum, defined a broad variety of technical specifications that should
be met by all *NFC*-systems (readers and tags). Therefore, within the *near
field communication* technology four different types of tags (*NFC Forum
Type 1-4* tags) exist. As for this, the *RFID* tag used for *Amiibos* is categorized as a *NFC Forum Type 2* tag.

3.1.1 *NFC Type 2* tags

NFC Type 2 tags are tags based on the *NFC-A* technology and furthermore are heavily oriented towards *MIFARE Ultralight* tags manufactured
by the company *NXP Semiconductors*. Hence they are merely used for saving data[24]. Several *Type 2* tags can operate simultaneously within a single
reader's range rather unproblematically, as anti-collision methods are used
for this.

Depending on the tag's memory size there are two different structures. On the one hand for a memory size equal to 64 bytes a static *EEPROM* (*Electrically Erasable Programmable Read-Only Memory*) structure and on the other hand a dynamic counterpart for bigger memory sizes is used. As for the data structure per se, the entire memory is divided into several blocks/pages, each containing exactly four bytes of data.

Static memory: As the memory size of tags, using static memory organization, is limited to 64 bytes only few access permissions need to be set.

Byte Number	0	1	2	3	Block
UID / Internal	Internal0	Internal1	Internal2	Internal3	0
Serial Number	Internal4	Internal5	Internal6	Internal7	1
Internal / Lock	Internal8	Internal9	Lock0	Lock1	2
CC	CC0	CC1	CC2	CC3	3
Data	Data0	Data1	Data2	Data3	4
Data	Data4	Data5	Data6	Data7	5
Data	Data8	Data9	Data10	Data11	6
Data	.	.	.	.	.
Data	.	.	.	.	.
Data	.	.	.	.	.
Data	.	.	.	.	.
Data	.	.	.	.	.
Data	.	.	.	.	15

Figure 3.1: Static memory organization of *Type 2* tags[26]

Therefore, exactly two bytes (the static lock bytes at page 2) are required to prevent further writing access. In order for this to work, every bit resembles an entire page and hence a logical 1_2 indicates a locked read-only content, whereas a logical 0_2 grants writing permission to the corresponding block address. The consecutive numbering from the second lock byte's most significant bit to the least significant bit and from the first lock byte's MSB to its fifth bit hereby individually represents the pages 15 to 3 in ascending order (see figure 3.2). The last three bits of static lock byte 1 furthermore enable whether some block groups can change their values or not.

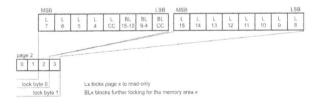

Figure 3.2: Static lock bytes 0 and 1[28]

Dynamic memory: *NFC* tags utilizing the dynamic memory organization mostly possess a memory size slightly bigger compared to their static counterparts. Hence further lock bytes are commonly used in order to properly cover the access states of the additional memory.

Byte Number	0	1	2	3	Block
UID / Internal	Internal0	Internal1	Internal2	Internal3	0
Serial Number	Internal4	Internal5	Internal6	Internal7	1
Internal / Lock	Internal8	Internal9	Lock0	Lock1	2
CC	CC0	CC1	CC2	CC3	3
Data	Data0	Data1	Data2	Data3	4
Data	Data4	Data5	Data6	Data7	5
Data	Data8	Data9	Data10	Data11	6
Data	.	.	.	.	.
Data	.	.	.	.	.
Data	.	.	.	.	.
Data	.	.	.	.	.
Data	.	.	.	.	n
Lock / Reserved	.	.	.	.	.
Lock / Reserved	.	.	.	.	.
Lock / Reserved	.	.	.	.	k

Figure 3.3: Dynamic memory organization of *Type 2* tags[26]

The dynamic lock bytes basically follow the same rules as the static lock bytes, but with the sole difference that for byte 1 and byte 2 every bit retrospectively represents an entire page group in this case. The third byte however will indicate bitwise, whether it is allowed to change the values of entire locked byte groups or not.

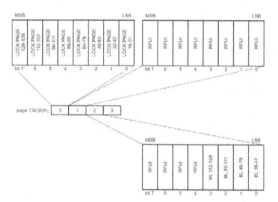

Figure 3.4: Dynamic lock bytes structure for the example of the *Amiibo's* *NTAG215*[28]

3.1.1.1 Capability Container (CC)

Despite the wide variety of *NFC* tags that currently exists, every system just needs to support a small subset. In order to accurately classify a handful of supported tags the *Capability Container* (*CC*) is used. Taking the example of *Type 2* tags, the *CC* is saved within the four bytes of block 3 and needs to follow certain rules. For this, the first byte is declared as the *NDEF Magic Number* and is always set to a constant value of $0xE1$. According to Paret et al. the *NDEF Magic Number* indicates that the *NFC* tag is a *NFC Forum* tag containing at least one *NDEF Message* stored within[30]. The second byte in turn gives further indication of the version of the used tag by means of the uniform *NFC Forum*-specification (the value XY matches the version number X.Y.). With the third byte the size of the useable data memory is defined as eight times the byte's value. Byte number 4 on the other hand gives further bits of information about the access states of the static memory. The most significant nibble (first four bits) therefore describes the reading permission and the only possible value for this is $0x0$, resulting in no restrictions. Whereas the least significant nibble (last four bits) represents the writing permission (e.g. $0xF$ asserts no writing permission at all). As mostly the field of application defines this value, it must not always match the actual state of the lock-bits.

3.1.1.2 TLV structure

Tag-Length-Value, or short *TLV*, are data structures representing all kinds of information and/or configuration parameter. For this, a *TLV*-pattern consists out of three basic fields (Tag-, Length- and Value-field), as it can be seen in figure 3.5 below.

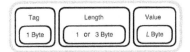

Tag	Length	Value
1 Byte	1 or 3 Byte	L Byte

Figure 3.5: Basic *TLV* structure[24]

The Tag-field contains a single byte, representing the type of the entire *TLV* block. The tag values from $0x04$ to $0xFC$ and $0xFF$ however are not possible in this context, as they are reserved for future use by the *NFC Forum*[26]. In strong comparison to the first field, the latter two must not always be present. Taking the case that the L-field however is available, it has one or three bytes stored within, either way in order to declare the actual length of the subsequent V-field. As a result, the V-field has a range from 0 to 254 (L-field is represented by one byte; excluding $0xFF$) or from 255 to

65534 (L-field is represented by three bytes; whereas the first one is set to $0xFF$ and the latter two define the actual length value) bytes, in order to store the current data within these.

- **NULL TLV**

  As the name already implies this *TLV*-structure is empty, resulting in an absence of the Length- and Value-field and in the Tag-value being $0x00$. The purpose of *NULL TLV*s is to mainly add a padding in between of memory areas or other *TLV*-structures. *NULL TLV*s and the *Terminator TLV* are furthermore the only *TLV* blocks within the entire *Type 2* tag that only consist out of one byte.

- **Lock Control TLV**

  TLV structures with a Tag-value of $0x01$ are declared as *Lock Control TLV*s. Additionally the Length-field inevitably has $0x03$ as its predefined value, resulting in the V-field having a length of three bytes. These three bytes furthermore indicate the position and the size of the locked bits, as well as the length of the locked area. Within the first byte of the V-field, the starting point (= byte address) of the locked bits is stored and can be calculated by the following formula:

  $$Byte\ Address = (MSB\ Nibble) * 2^{(bytes\ per\ page)} + (LSB\ Nibble)$$

  The middle byte gives further information about the amount of locked bits and the length of the locked area is given by the V-field's least significant byte.

- **Memory Control TLV**

  As the *Lock Control TLV* is used for the tag's locked data, the *Memory Control TLV*, as the former's counterpart, clearly defines the tag's reserved memory. For this, these structures strongly resemble each other, with the sole difference that the Tag-field has a constant value of $0x02$. All *Lock Control TLV*s and *Memory Control TLV*s need to be saved within the *NFC* tag before any *NDEF Message TLV* or *Proprietary TLV*.

- **NDEF Message TLV**

  This *TLV*-structure has a Tag-value of $0x03$ and has, rather than the former mentioned pendants, a Length-field without a predefined value. For this, the Value-field contains L bits of information in the *NFC Data Exchange Format (NDEF)*. At least one *NDEF Message TLV* needs to be stored within an entire *Type 1 NFC* tag, but however does not necessarily need to be available within *Type 2 NFC* tags at all.

- **Proprietary TLV**
  *Proprietary TLV*s always begin with a Tag-value of $0xFD$ and, as by definition, store proprietary data within the Value-field.

- **Terminator TLV**
  If present, the last *TLV* within the *NFC* tag will be the so-called *Terminator TLV*. This structure has neither a Length- nor a Value-field and hence only consists of a single $0xFE$ byte as Tag-field. Its sole purpose is to mark the end of all *TLV*-structures in the memory.

3.1.1.3 Commands

As the main purpose of *NFC Type 2* tags is to store data within, only three basic commands are needed to cover all use cases: *READ* ($0x30$), *WRITE* ($0xA2$) & *SECTOR_SELECT* ($0x9370/0x9570$). The *READ*-command always returns 16 bytes at once, whereas with the *WRITE*-command only four bytes per iteration can be saved back to the tag. Writing- and reading-permissions are limited to a maximum memory size of one kilobyte. As a result, the third command, namely *SECTOR_SELECT*, is used in order to access another - also one kilobyte sized - sector.

The *ISO/IEC 14443* standard declares further commands in order to establish or pause a connection. In addition to the existing commands, it is up to the manufacturer to establish new ones. Therefore, taking the example of the *NFC* tag used for *Amiibos*, the following additional commands are available:

Command	Value	Description
GET_VERSION	$0x60$	With this command the version information for the specific tag type is received (ref 3.1.2).
FAST_READ	$0x3A$	By providing additional start and end page addresses, the scope within is returned at once.
COMP_WRITE	$0xA0$	The *COMPATIBILITY_WRITE* command is implemented to guarantee interoperability with other infrastructures[28].
READ_CNT	$0x39$	The *NFC* tag's counter value is returned by applying this command (ref 3.1.2).
PWD_AUTH	$0x1B$	By providing the valid password as a parameter, the password protected *NFC* tag's memory can get accessed to. The password authentication acknowledge is the actual return value (ref 3.2).
READ_SIG	$0x3C$	With this command the tag's specific 32-byte signature is returned (ref 3.2.1.3).

Table 3.1: Table showing the *Amiibo*'s *NFC* tag's specific commands

3.1.2   *Amiibo* Data Page Table

As already mentioned beforehand, the *NFC* tag stored within *Amiibos* is based on the *NFC Forum Type 2* standard and furthermore, in more detail, is a product named *NTAG215* by the manufacturer *NXP Semiconductors*. Despite the many standards defined for *NFC Forum Type 2* tags, the *NTAG215* within *Amiibos* does not necessarily fit all of these schemes. Therefore, a detailed table plus description, based upon the own findings of analyzing many *Amiibo* data (for reference see A.3), is listed below.

Access	Page	Byte 1	Byte 2	Byte 3	Byte 4
Locked	0	UID	UID	UID	Check byte
Locked	1	UID	UID	UID	UID
Locked	2	Check byte	Reserved for internal usage	2 static lock bytes	
Locked	3	One time programmable area			
Unlocked	4	NFC counter			Reserved for internal usage
Unlocked	5 - 12	Saved *Amiibo* data			
Locked	13 - 31	Tag specific locked data			
Unlocked	32 - 129	Saved *Amiibo* data			
Locked	130	3 dynamic lock bytes			Reserved for future usage
Locked	131 - 132	Configuration			
Not readable	133	32 bit password			
Not readable	134	2 bytes password verification (PACK)		Reserved for future usage	

Table 3.2: Data page table of *Amiibo NFC* tags

The *Amiibos'* embedded *NFC* tag has a total capacity of 540 bytes, organized in 135 pages with each containing four bytes. In order to clearly distinct the tag within an electromagnetic field, an **unique identifier (UID)** of seven byte length is saved in the first three bytes of page 0 and in the entire page 1. In accordance to *ISO/IEC 14443-3* the first byte of the **UID** always holds the predefined manufacturer identifier[28]. Therefore, as for the example of *NXP Semiconductors*, all *Amiibos'* serial numbers start with 0x04. Additionally two **check bytes** are located at the last byte of page address 0 and at the first byte of page 2 in order to check the correctness of the read **UID**. For this, the first **check byte** is calculated by the *Boolean* XOR operation of CT $UID1$ $UID2$ $UID3$, whereas *check byte* number two is defined by $UID4$ $UID5$ $UID6$ $UID7$. In this context CT stands for a *cascade tag* with a constant value of 0x88, indicating that the **UID** is not yet completed. The second byte of page 2 possesses a constant value of 0x48 and is reserved for internal usage according to the public *NTAG215* data sheet. Due to being pre-programmed and write protected while in production, the first three page addresses are constantly locked as a matter of fact.

The **one time programmable area** located at page 3 however does not fit the usual *Type 2* tags' *Capability Container* standard. Instead of the typical *NDEF Magic Number* of $0xE1$, a constant value of $0xF1$ is defined for all *Amiibos*. As *Nintendo* was not capable of delivering a large amount of certain *Amiibo* figures at a given point, some figurines have been reworked over the time for another release. The second byte on page address 3 therefore gives further indication about the *Amiibos*' internal version numbers. Figures that have not been edited and re-released so far feature a version number of 1.0. represented by a hexadecimal value of $0x10$, whereas restored products hereby possess a higher value.

The **2 static lock bytes** are set to a constant value of $0x0FE0$ in hexadecimal and $0000\ 1111\ 1110\ 0000_2$ in binary. As a result and according to the configuration defined for *NFC Type 2 tags*, the *Capability Container* at page address 3 and the pages 13 to 15 are locked and their access states cannot be changed retrospectively. Moreover the **3 dynamic lock bytes** possess an unchangeable hex value of $0x01000F$ ($0000\ 0001\ 0000\ 0000\ 0000\ 1111_2$ in binary) and will therefore lock - as described in 3.1.1 - the pages ranged from address 16 to 31.

As the *NDEF Magic Number* of the *Capability Container* already lead to the assumption that no *NDEF Message* is stored within the entire *NFC* tag, this speculation is further proven to be true by analyzing the actual proprietary **saved *Amiibo* data**. The pages 5 to 12 and 32 to 129 nevertheless do not contain any other *TLV*-structure either. Page addresses ranged from 13 to 31 on the other hand are locked and possess **tag specific data** that is overall different for all *Amiibos*; even for the same character model these values strongly differ. However, most striking for this section is that the blocks 21 and 22 define the video game character, the game series and the *Amiibo* series represented by the *Amiibo* per se (for reference see table 3.3).

Page	Nibble 1	Nibble 2	Nibble 3	Nibble 4	Nibble 5	Nibble 6	Nibble 7	Nibble 8
21		Game series		Character index	Character variation		*Amiibo* type	
22		Internal index for enumerating all *Amiibo* models			*Amiibo* series			

Table 3.3: Structure of page 21 & 22 indicating the represented *Amiibo* series, video game character and the corresponding game series

Page 21's first 12 bits define a certain video game series and the following nibble indicates a video game character taken from the former (see table 3.4). In most cases these 4 bits are clearly sufficient in order to precisely index a video gaming character within the corresponding series. But however this does not apply for *Nintendos Pokémon* franchise at all. At the time of writing a total amount of 721 so-called *pocket monsters* exists, whereas the 2 aforesaid bytes need to get looked at in their entirety. For this, the *Pokémon* are classified by their internal consecutive numbering starting with $0x1901$ for monster number #001: *Bulbasaur* and ranging to $0x1BD1$ for the last entry of *Pokémon* #721. As *Nintendo* exhibits a broad variety of characters, some of them bear a strong resemblance to each other or are even duplicates. Therefore, character analogies like *Link* and *Toon Link* (from the *The Legend of Zelda*-series) or *Super Mario* and *Dr. Mario* (from the *Super Mario Bros.*-series) are represented by the same four bits for the character model, but can rather be differentiated by the third byte of page address 21. The least significant byte of this page identifies the kind of the *Amiibo*. Therefore, *Amiibos* based upon plastic figurines possess a constant value of $0x00$, *Amiibo* cards hereby state $0x01$ and the yarn *Amiibos* of the *Yoshi's Woolly World Collection* are declared by $0x02$.

Game Series	Nibble 1	Nibble 2	Nibble 3
Animal Crossing Series	$0x0$	$0x1$	$0x8$
Chibi-Robo Series*	TBA	TBA	TBA
Donkey Kong Series	$0x0$	$0x0$	$0x0$
Duck Hunt Series	$0x0$	$0x7$	$0x8$
F-Zero Series	$0x0$	$0x6$	$0x0$
Fire Emblem Series	$0x2$	$0x1$	$0x0$
Game & Watch Series	$0x0$	$0x7$	$0x8$
Kid Icarus Series	$0x0$	$0x7$	$0x4$
Kirby Series	$0x1$	$0xF$	$0x0$
Mega Man Series	$0x3$	$0x4$	$0x8$
Metroid Series	$0x0$	$0x5$	$0xC$
Mother/Earthbound Series	$0x2$	$0x2$	$0x8$
Nintendo Mii Series	$0x0$	$0x7$	$0xC$
Pac-Man Series	$0x3$	$0x3$	$0x4$
Pikmin Series	$0x0$	$0x6$	$0x4$
Pokémon Series**	$0x1$ / $0x1^+$	$0x9$ / $0xB^+$	$0x0$ / $0xD^+$
Punch-Out!! Series	$0x0$	$0x6$	$0xC$
R.O.B. Series	$0x0$	$0x7$	$0x8$
Shovel Knight Series*	TBA	TBA	TBA
Sonic the Hedgehog Series	$0x3$	$0x2$	$0x0$
Splatoon Series	$0x0$	$0x8$	$0x0$
Star Fox Series	$0x0$	$0x5$	$0x8$
Street Fighter Series*	TBA	TBA	TBA
Super Mario Bros. Series	$0x0$	$0x0$	$0x0$
The Legend of Zelda Series	$0x0$	$0x1$	$0x0$
Wario Series	$0x0$	$0x0$	$0x0$
Wii-Fit Series	$0x0$	$0x7$	$0x0$
Xenoblade Chronicles Series	$0x2$	$0x2$	$0x4$
Yoshi Series	$0x0$	$0x0$	$0x0$
* No *Amiibo* of this game series has yet been published.			
** Currently indexed from $0x1901$ (*Pokémon* #001) to $0x1BD1$ (#721)			

Table 3.4: Table showing the different values of the game series of the corresponding *Amiibo* character

As the number of released *Amiibo* figurines is constantly growing, *Nintendo* therefore keeps track of them by allocating a steadily incrementing index to each model. This number can hence be extracted from the first two bytes of page 22. The next two bytes then are reserved for the *Amiibo* series (for reference of all values see table 3.5 below).

Amiibo Series	Byte 1	Byte 2
Super Smash Bros. Collection	0x00	0x02
Super Mario Bros. Collection	0x01	0x02
Yoshi's Woolly World Collection	0x03	0x02
Splatoon Collection	0x04	0x02
Animal Crossing Collection	0x05	0x02
Chibi-Robo Collection*	TBA	TBA
Super Mario 30th Anniversary Collection*	TBA	TBA
Skylander-Crossover Collection*	TBA	TBA
* These *Amiibo* collections are not yet published.		

Table 3.5: Table showing the different values of the *Amiibo* series

The tags' predefined **configurations** are stored at the page addresses 131 and 132. *NXP Semiconductors* introduced the new feature of *UID/NFC Counter ASCII mirroring* with their latest product line of *NTAG21x*, which the *Amiibos*' tags are based upon. This feature would allow saving the **UID** and/or a counter value (for the amount of successful writing accesses) into the *NFC* tag's memory in *ASCII* code, basically in order to allow an easier usage within *NDEF Messages*. Since the *NFC* tag stored within *Amiibos* however does not hold any *NDEF Messages*, the aforementioned feature is naturally disabled. This can be further confirmed by looking at the first nibble of page 131's first byte and at byte number 3 of the implied block. Typically the first two bits indicate whether this feature is enabled (01_2-11_2) or not (00_2) and the following two bits, in combination with byte 3, clearly define the byte and page position for the beginning of the *ASCII* mirroring. Therefore, with a constant value of 0x000000, the mirroring feature is proven to be disabled. As only the first byte of page 132 is used (all other bytes are yet reserved for future usage), this value is thus set to an invariable value of 0x5F (01011111_2 in binary) for all *Amiibos*. Due to the second bit being 1_2, the entire configuration pages are permanently locked against write access. With the forth bit possessing also a value of 1_2, the **NFC counter** feature is therefore enabled. Every time the *NFC* tag's memory is written to, the 24 bit counter value, which is stored within the first three bytes of page address 4, is automatically increased by one. As no defaults exist, all *Amiibos* hereby initially start fresh out of the box with a predefined value of 0xA50000. In case the stored data will be reset, a random number between 0x1000 and

$0xFFFF$ is added to the **NFC counter s** value. Once the maximum value of $0xFFFFFF$ was reached, this value would not be able to change any longer.

3.2 Password

In additional reference to the *Amiibo* data page table (as described above in chapter 3.1.2), data pages which are declared as locked cannot get overridden, whereas unlocked ones can easily be changed. In order to avoid unauthorized memory alterations though, the *NTAG215* can be secured with a **32 bit password** stored at page address 133. The last byte of page 131 therefore defines a page address as the starting point from which the password verification is required as an ongoing/continuing fashion. If the page address however is set to an index higher than the actual tag's length, the password protection will be disabled after all. Not only the writing access can be protected by the password, but rather can the *NFC* tag become prohibited from being read without a valid authorization too. As *Amiibos* however have a predefined bit of 0_2 as the most significant bit of page 132's first byte, the password is solely needed to gain writing permission. Mostly in order to prevent brute-force, the *NFC* tag also possesses a limitation for negative password verification attempts stored at the last three bits of aforesaid byte. Converted from the binary value of 111_2 (page 132's first byte is constantly $0x5F$), the tag's memory can be tried to get accessed by exactly seven times before the tag will inevitably get locked permanently. Once the authorization succeeds however, this counter will immediately become reset. Neither the password nor the dedicated **2 byte password authentication acknowledge** (**PACK**) can be read directly from the *NFC* tag. Therefore, instead of transmitting the real value, a dummy entry of $0x00$ is replied as a return value for every requested read command of the related pages.

Based upon the latest cryptographic standards and in order to increase the overall system security, *elliptic curves* are used for the *Amiibos'* passwords and signatures.

3.2.1 *Elliptic curve cryptography*

With the fast evolving advances in technology and the vastly growing data rates as a direct consequence, cryptography systems need to adapt to this situation as well. Hence the history of cryptography can be categorized into two eras: the classic and the modern era. Therefore, cryptological techniques evolved from security schemes that are based upon letters (e.g. the *Caesar cipher* where every letter in the alphabet is switched with a different one) to the actual forms of number-based systems. Besides the well-known examples of the *RSA* algorithm or the *Di e-Hellman key exchange* algorithm, *elliptic curve cryptography* is a more modern and more powerful approach.

3.2.1.1 Definition of *elliptic curves*

A polynomial is by mathematical means mostly an expression with variables and coefficients. Two basic examples hereof are $x^2 + y^2 = r^2$ (which, plotted over $\mathbb{R}$, results in a circle) and one of its numerous variations with coefficients $a * x^2 + b * y^2 = c^2$ (depicted as an ellipse). By the means of these illustrations other types of graphs (due to their shapes later on mostly referred to as curves) can be formed.

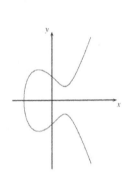

Figure 3.6: *Elliptic curve* example of the equation $y^2 = x^3 - 3x + 3$ (over $\mathbb{R}$)[29]

Hence according to the definition taken from Paar et Pelzl[29], an *elliptic curve* is a special type of polynomial equation for which the set of all pairs $(x, y) \in \mathbb{Z}$ fulfill

$$y^2 \equiv x^3 + a * x + b \text{ where } a, b \in \mathbb{Z}$$

and the condition $4 * a^3 + 27 * b^2 \neq 0$. The latter formula will cause the *elliptic curve* to be non-singular, meaning that geometrically the graph has no self-intersections or isolated points, and that in every point a tangent would be clearly distinct. Whatsoever *elliptic curves* are no ellipses after all, but they received their name due to their usage for determining the circumference of the latter.

Most noticeable for the plotted *elliptic curve* is that the outcome is symmetric with respect to the x-axis. This is a direct result from the fact that for every value of x_i on the *elliptic curve* a total amount of two solutions exists: $\pm\sqrt{x_i^3 + a * x_i + b}$. Furthermore, due to the *elliptic curve* being non-singular and based on a cubic function (as the equation contains x^3), there is only one intersection of the graph with the x-axis. By solving the function for $y = 0$, one solution in $\mathbb{R}$ (this is directly depicted as the intersection with the x-axis) and further two complex solutions are found. As the coordinate system however is based upon $\mathbb{R}^2$, the latter two are logically not showing up in the plot.

3.2.1.2   Computing with *elliptic curves*

As the *elliptic curve cryptography* is an important part of the modern era, it is also founded on the idea of a two keys cryptosystem (*public key cryptographic system*). The first one, referred to as a *public key*, is solely used to encrypt the data and as a result, it may as well be known to anyone. While the latter *private key* in turn is required to decrypt the data again, it shall be kept secret at any price. In order for a *public key cryptographic system* to work long-term (it shall be secure for as long as possible), a set of algorithms, which are easy to process in one direction but by comparison are rather difficult to undo, needs to be found. Algorithms featuring the aforesaid characteristic are most commonly known as *trapdoor functions*. Therefore, finding a good *trapdoor function* is the quintessence of a secure *public key cryptographic system*, whereas it is hence considered to be more secure the bigger the spread between the difficulty in going one direction in the *trapdoor function* and undoing it will be.

Taking the example of *elliptic curve cryptography*, the underlying *trapdoor function* has a geometric interpretation too: the addition of two points $P = (x_1|y_1)$ and $Q = (x_2|y_2)$ on the curve. For this, a line is drawn directly through both P and Q and, as a result, a point as the third intersection of the line with the curve is obtained. Once this point is mirrored along the x-axis, $R = [(x_1 + x_2)|(y_1 + y_2)]$ is obtained by the definition of the method of **Point Addition** (for reference see figure 3.7 below). In case P is however equal to Q, a tangent line instead of a secant is drawn through the point. Then again the freshly obtained intersection with the *elliptic curve* is mirrored alongside the x-axis in order to receive the result $R = 2 * P$ of **Point Doubling** P (refer to figure 3.7 once again).

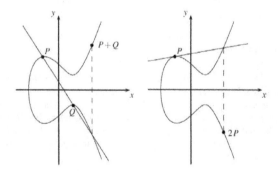

Figure 3.7: Point Addition (left) and **Point Doubling** (right) for *elliptic curves*[29]

In a cryptosystem these geometric constructions cannot be performed however, whereas this needs to be replaced by analytic expressions and formulas. According to the equation of an *elliptic curve*, the y-value is always inversely proportional to the x-value. As a result, the y-value can easily grow towards $\pm\ $. Computers however often have some difficulties with processing these arbitrary large numbers. Therefore, in order to ensure that the numbers dealt with are not getting too big, a maximum number is chosen. Once if any calculation results in a number equal to or larger than the predefined maximum, it will get cropped to fit the valid range (this is achieved by computing the result modulo the maximum value). For this, the maximum is mostly picked to be a prime number p, as the *elliptic curve* (in this case called a *prime curve*) therefore will receive better cryptographic properties[6]. As the equation of the *elliptic curve* is hence also limited to a certain field instead of $\mathbb{R}^2$, the following analytical expressions for the methods of point addition and point doubling can be yield:

Elliptic Curve Point Addition and Point Doubling[29]

$$x_3 = s^2 - x_1 - x_2 \bmod p$$
$$y_3 = s * (x_1 - x_3) - y_1 \bmod p$$

where

$$s = \begin{cases} \frac{y_2 - y_1}{x_2 - x_1} \bmod p & \text{if P} \neq \text{Q (point addition)} \\ \frac{3*x_1^2 + a}{2*y_1} \bmod p & \text{if P} = \text{Q (point doubling)} \end{cases}$$

The variable s in this context stands for the slope of the secant through P and Q for point addition, or the slope of the tangent of P in the case of point doubling.

As another direct consequence to this limitation, the *elliptic curve* receives an order q. Due to the fact that for each point addition/doubling result the x- and y-coordinates will conclusively be computed with a modulo p operation, the later outcome might be identical to an already formerly obtained value. For example, this means that if a point P on the curve had already been point doubled several times (e.g. $35P$) and the calculation has yet to be computed once again ($35P + P$), the result might be of the same value as the original point. In case this assumption asserts true, the amount of operations needed to accomplish this behavior (in this example: 36) is considered to be the order q of an *elliptic curve*.

3.2.1.2.1 Key Exchange

For the *private* and *public keys* of an *elliptic curve* cryptosystem, one of the aforesaid curve equations (one that is limited by a predefined maximum value) is required, as well as a randomly chosen public point P_{random} on the curve. Yet another randomly chosen number *priv*, one that however is smaller than the actual order of the used *elliptic curve*, marks the first *private key*. Moreover the second *private key* is declared as another point $P_{private}$ that is part of the curve. With a total amount of two *private keys*, two *public keys* can be generated as well. For this, the first one is the point P_{public_1} generated by a continuous point doubling of point adding P_{random} and $P_{private}$ for exactly *priv*-times $(P_{public_1} = priv * (P_{random} + P_{private}))$. In turn the second *public key* is the direct result of *priv*-times point doubling $P_{private}$ $(P_{public_2} = priv * P_{private})$.

The result of point doubling any of the two *public keys priv*-times can be used to derive a *session key* $P_{session}$. As $P_{session}$ is part of the curve too, the x- and y-coordinates can be computed with the equation at anytime in case one of them is known. Thus in particular only one of these two coordinates (mostly the x-value) should be used for the derivation.

3.2.1.2.2 Message Encryption

For encrypting a message using an *elliptic curve*, every point that only consists out of whole number coordinates represents a specific character. (Such a curve is depicted below as figure 3.8.) By enumerating every point plus the mirrored counterparts, a character code table can be formed.

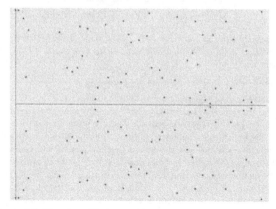

Figure 3.8: Plot of an *elliptic curve* that is wrapped around the maximum and where only whole number coordinates are displayed as points[6]

Every character within the encryption message is then mapped to the corresponding entry defined in the obtained table. Then again for encrypting each of these points $P_{message}$ to a pair of cipher points E_1 and E_2, a further random number $rand$ which however is different for every operation is needed. On the one hand E_1 is generated by point doubling the former point P_{random} $rand$-times ($E_1 = rand * P_{random}$). E_2 on the other hand is a bit more complex to compute, as $E_2 = P_{message} + (priv + rand) * P_{public_1} - rand * P_{public_2} + P_{session}$. After the entire encryption process, in order to convert all the characters back into a human-readable form, every tuple of E_1 and E_2 needs to get mapped once again to the corresponding characters.

3.2.1.2.3   Message Decryption

For a successful decryption of the message, the last step in the entire encryption process needs to be undone first. Therefore, every pair of four characters needs to be reverted to their point representations E_1 and E_2 in the character code table. By applying $P_{message} = E_2 - (priv * E_1 + priv * P_{public_1} + P_{session})$ the cipher point tuple is then converted to another point on the *elliptic curve*. Once this result is mapped to the corresponding character within the table again, the original decrypted symbol is finally obtained.

3.2.1.3   Signatures

Digital signatures are used to provide data origin authentication, data integrity and non-repudiation. Hence these schemes are commonly used to sign certificates in order to bind together an entity and its *public key*. According to Hankerson et al a signature scheme is hence said to be secure if it is existentially unforgeable by a computationally bounded adversary. Therefore, by obtaining signatures of any message it should not be possible to reproduce a new valid signature[18]. Due to the absence of strong attacks against *elliptic curve cryptography* this system is often used for applying digital signatures. Furthermore, shorter bit lengths, compared to other cryptosystems, can be used. As a matter of fact this results in shorter processing time, but would also lead to shorter signatures. Hence the most widely used *elliptic curve*-based signature scheme, namely the *Elliptic Curve Digital Signature Algorithm (ECDSA)*, has been standardized by the *American National Standards Institute (ANSI)* in 1998[29].

ECDSA signature generation

For generating a signature using the *Elliptic Curve Digital Signature Algorithm* (algorithm 3.1), an *elliptic curve* limited over a certain field is required. Therefore, the defined maximum p, as well as the resulting order q of the curve, are two basic parameters for the algorithm. The process furthermore needs the coefficients a and b that are defined by the used *elliptic curve* equation of $y^2 = x^3 \pm ax \pm b$. In order to prohibit adversary from reproducing new valid signatures, the point $P_{private}$ on the curve and the random number $priv$, as the two *private keys*, are also required.

An *ECDSA* signature contains a pair of integers r and s with both possessing the same bit length as the order q of the utilized *elliptic curve*. In order to get to these results, an ephemeral key $k_E \in \mathbb{N}$ as a random number in between the interval $]0, q[$ has to be chosen first of all. By applying a point duplication of $P_{private}$ for exactly k_E times, a new point R located on the curve is obtained. The absolute value of the point's x-coordinate modulo q hereby marks the value of r respectively. In case r is by now set to 0, this procedure however has to be redone again. By applying a *hash function* to the message, the received hash is a compressed version that serves as a further representative of the message. During the signing process s is then computed by dividing the addition of the former hash and $priv * r$ with the key k_E modulo q.

Algorithm 3.1: *ECDSA* signature generation

INPUT: *Elliptic curve* domain parameters (maximum p, order q, coefficients a & b, point $P_{private}$), *hash function* H, private key $priv$, message m
OUTPUT: Digital signature (r, s)

1: **do**
2:      Choose an ephemeral key k_E with $0 < k_E < q$ and $k_E \in \mathbb{N}$
3:      Compute the point $R = (k_E * P_{private})$ modulo p
4:      Compute $r = |x_R|$ modulo q
5: **while** $(r \neq 0)$
6: Get the *hash* $h = H(m)$ of the message m using the function H
7: Compute $s = (\frac{h + priv * r}{k_E})$ modulo q
8: Return the signature (r, s)

ECDSA signature verification

Unlike the signature generation process that should be kept private at all costs, verifying a signature (r, s) should be possible anytime for anyone. Hence no *private keys* are required as input for the algorithm 3.2, but rather their *public key* counterparts are used. Furthermore, the used *elliptic curve* has to be clearly distinct by the coefficients a and b, the maximum p and the order q.

Taking the case that neither r nor s is within the range of the natural numbers $\mathbb{N}$ or the interval $[1, q - 1]$, the signature is already rejected in the first place. Otherwise the auxiliary value w as the result of s^{-1} modulo q is then computed. Further two variables u_1 and u_2 are obtained afterwards by multiplying w with either the hashed message $h = H(m)$ or r in combination with another modulo q operation. By point doubling P_{random} for u_1 times and adding $u_2 * P_{public_2}$ to the former outcome, the most important part of the entire verification process, the point P_{verify} on the curve, is received.

If P_{verify} is however considered to be located somewhere near infinity due to the high value of the x- or y-coordinate, the verification will be canceled with a negative result. Lastly, only in case the absolute value of P_{verify}'s x-coordinate modulo q is equal to r modulo q, the signature can be verified as a valid one.

Algorithm 3.2: *ECDSA* signature verification

INPUT: *Elliptic curve* domain parameters (maximum p, order q, coefficients a & b, point P_{random}), *hash function* H, public key $P_{public2}$, message m, signature (r, s)

OUTPUT: Acceptance or rejection of the signature

1: **if** $((r$ or $s \notin \mathbb{N})$ or $(r$ or s are not in the interval $[1, q - 1]))$ **then**
2:     Return ("Reject the signature")
3: **else**
4:     Get the *hash* $h = H(m)$ of the message m using the function H
5:     Compute auxiliary value $w = s^{-1}$ modulo q
6:     Compute auxiliary value $u_1 = w * h$ modulo q
7:     Compute auxiliary value $u_2 = w * r$ modulo q
8:     Compute $P_{verify} = u_1 * P_{random} + u_2 * P_{public2}$
9:     **if** $(P_{verify} \equiv)$ **then**
10:         Return ("Reject the signature")
11:     **else**
12:         Compute $v = |x_{P_{verify}}|$ modulo q
13:         The verification follows from:
14:         **if** $(v \not\equiv (r$ modulo $q))$ **then**
15:             Return ("Reject the signature")
16:         **else**   . $v \equiv (r$ modulo $q)$
17:             Return ("Accept the signature")
18:         **end if**
19:     **end if**
20: **end if**

3.2.2 *Elliptic curve cryptography* and *Amiibos*

Finding an *elliptic curve* with good cryptographic properties is a rather hard task. Therefore, several recommended standards exist for an overall increased security. The *elliptic curve* that is used for *Amiibos* is one of these, namely a 128-bit standardized *elliptic curve* over a maximum p (*secp128r1*)[31]. For this, the curve equation is predefined as $y^2 = x^3 + a*x + b$ with a set to a constant value of $0xFFFFFFFD\ FFFFFFFF\ FFFF$-$FFFF\ FFFFFFFC$ (approx. $3.4028 * 10^{38}$) and b set to $0xE87579C1$ 10-$79F43D\ D824993C\ 2CEE5ED3$ (approx. $3.0899 * 10^{38}$). As 128 bit are used for every numeric parameter, the maximum $p = 0xFFFFFFFD\ FFFF$-$FFFF\ FFFFFFFF\ FFFFFFFF$ (approx. $3.4028 * 10^{38}$) is only slightly beyond the maximum attainable value of 2^{128}. The randomly chosen public point P_{random} is also predefined by ($0x161FF752\ 8B899B2D\ 0C28607C$ $A52C5B86,\ 0xCF5AC839\ 5BAFEB13\ C02DA292\ DDED7A83$) which for better clearance is approximately ($2.9409 * 10^{37}, 2.7562 * 10^{38}$). Therefore, calculating the order q of the *elliptic curve* results in $0xFFFFFFFE$ 00-000000 $75A30D1B$ $9038A115$ (approx. $3.4028 * 10^{38}$).

As already stated above, for the case of *Amiibos elliptic curve cryptography* is on the one hand used for the 32-bit password generation, as well as for the signing process of the embedded *NFC* tag's data on the other hand. The *public key* for every *Amiibo* is defined by "NXP NTAG21x 2013" which means that for each figure the exact same two *private keys* $priv$ and $P_{private}$ are used. However, by the utilization of a *NFC sniffer* for surveilling and tracing the connection between an *Amiibo* and the gaming console, these logs revealed that the password is completely different for every tag. For an example, a *Yoshi Amiibo* had the password $0x1C583C4C$, whereas a *Villager Amiibo*'s password was set to $0xC482C44C$ and a *Super Mario* figurine had a value of $0x2CB2E8A5$ as its password. Thus this leads to the assumption that for the password encryption the *Amiibos*' UIDs are then used as the messages. This would apply for the signatures as well, as they are also diverse for all *Amiibos*.

3.3 Communication protocol

Besides the many standards that exist for the *NFC*-technology, the structures and the flow of an established connection between *NFC*-reader and one or several tags need to be clearly defined too. For this purpose these schemes are categorized into separate layers, based on the *Open Systems Interconnection Reference Model*. Communication functions are hence divided into following seven layers (enumerated from 1 to 7): *Physical Layer, Data Link Layer, Network Layer, Transport Layer, Session Layer, Presentation Layer & Application Layer*. A communication over *NFC* usually involves three or four of the above mentioned layers (see figure 3.9).

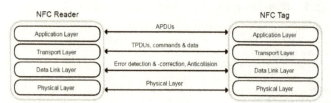

Figure 3.9: Typical protocol stack of *ISO/IEC 7816 NFC* smart cards (the *Application Layer* is not used for tags based on the *ISO 14443* standard)[24]

In this context the *Physical Layer* (layer 1) mostly defines the electrical and physical specifications of the data connection. Therefore, the transmission of raw bit streams over a physical medium and furthermore the protocol for establishing and terminating a connection between two nodes is set up here. Errordetection and -correction, besides the required anti-collision methods, are part of the *Data Link Layer*. Within the *Transport Layer*, the data transfer is declared (as already stated in section 2.2.2.2) and thus the way of encoding the obtained bits of information for the used signaling technology. On the same level the data packages wrapped in so-called *TPDU*s (*transport protocol data units*) are then bit-/block-wise transmitted. Only *NFC* tags based on the *ISO/IEC 7816* standards will use the *Application Layer* as a part of the connection. At this level the application specific requests and responses are hereby grouped to *APDU*s (*application protocol data units*) within the former transport protocol data units.

3.3.1 Transmission protocol

For the block-wise and asynchronous transmission protocol three block types as transport protocol data units exist: *I-block*, *R-block* & *S-block*.

- **I-block** (*information-block*): This block is either used to store data for the *Application Layer* (later on set to *APDU*s) or it can be used to exchange a command with the *NFC* tag and save its response.

- **R-block** (*receive-block*): This block indicates the exchange of either a positive or a negative acknowledgment of the transmission.

- **S-block** (*supervisory-block*): This block contains parameters and controls regarding the transmission protocol per se.

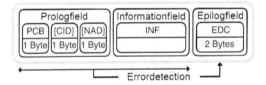

Figure 3.10: Block structure of the transmission protocol[24]

Then again each block consists of a prolog-field, an optional information-field and last but not least an epilog-field (for reference see figure 3.10 above). The prolog-field in turn is further divided into one to three bytes.

Hereby is the first byte the only non-optional one and is declared as the *protocol control byte* (*PCB*) marking the type of the block. Especially for *R-blocks* it depicts a possibly occurred error code. However, taking the case of a used *S-block*, the value is set to a communication control command or its result. Throughout the latter two bytes, several tags can be communicated with simultaneously (set by the optional *card identification byte CID*), whereas these tags are all differentiated over the *node address* (*NAD*) byte. For *R-blocks* the following information-field is not available. Otherwise it is always present and holds on the one hand data for the *Application Layer* (for *I-blocks* only) or on the other hand it stores parameters and controls for the transmission protocol (for *S-blocks*). At last in the epilog-field the two byte errordetection code is saved as a checksum generated by the preceded bytes.

With the aid of this protocol the *NFC*-reader and the tag can communicate with each other. For this, the active partner (the reader) transmits a request to the passive partner (the tag). Later on the response is returned to the reader again. Thus this procedure of exchanging *I-blocks* of *TPDU*s happens in an ongoing and alternating fashion. The system is therefore said to operate in a *half-duplex* mode. As the *NFC* tag is now either based on an *ISO/IEC 14443* or on an *ISO/IEC 7186* standard, two different information-field structures are hereby differentiated.

For *ISO/IEC 14443* based units, the information-field hereby starts with a length definition and further contains a two byte command, as well as the passed on data. According to the set command bytes, altogether six different request-response pairs are defined:

- **Attribute Request/Response**
  The *Attribute Request* serves as a connection buildup for the connection between *NFC*-reader and the transceiver. A *REQA* (*request attribute*) command with a predefined command byte of $0x26$ is sent out to all *NFC* tags within reach and invites the ones that did not already reply earlier to respond. In case no tag responds, the command is send over and over again. Otherwise an *ATQA* (*answer to request*) block is returned.

- **Parameter Selection Request/Response**
  Right after the reader has received the *ATQA* block an anti-collision method (ref 2.2.2.3) is triggered in order to receive the tag's UID. Depending on the length of the UID several *SELECT* commands are sent and therefore in turn the equal amount of *SAK* (*select acknowledge*) responses are returned. Each of these request-result pairs is referred to as a cascade level. Finally the tag gets activated whenever the last

SAK announces (by the absence of an extra returned cascading byte) that no further UID bytes are available.

- **Deselect Request/Response**
  Once the tag received the former state of activation, it processes all inquiries received from the reader unit. By casting a $0x5000$ *HLTA* command, the tag will get deselected. This means that it does not respond to any requests any longer.

- **Wakeup Request/Response**
  As the deselected state, evoked by the former deselect request, is equal to a special type of awaiting state, the *NFC* tag can always become reactivated again by the composite ($0x52$ & UID) *WUPA wake-up* command. Tags in an active, idle or awaiting state do no longer respond to a *REQA* request. These states have thus the further purpose to easily distinguish between already processed tags and ones yet to get selected. Just like for the attribute request, an *ATQA* response is supposed to be the return value and hence initializes an anti-collision method as well as the *SELECT* cascade blocks.

- **Release Request/Response**
  In order to completely deactivate a tag and to entirely close the connection, the release request is used. After transmitting the release response, the tag is reverted to its initial state before the first activation. A new *REQA* request is then needed in order to enable the communication again.

- **Data Exchange Protocol Request/Response**
  While the reader possesses an established connection to the *NFC* tag, these two units can exchange data with *data exchange protocol* request-response pairs. All other commands that were not yet mentioned, just like *READ*, *WRITE*, or the ones individually declared by the manufacturer (examples for the *NTAG215* of *Amiibos* are listed in table 3.1), fall within this scope.

For *NFC* tags that use *ISO/IEC 7186* standards, the transferred data is encapsulated in *APDU*s and is filled within the information-fields. Taking the case that an application protocol data unit is however too big to fit into only one block, it is split and transmitted in several parts. In this scenario the exchange sequence is also set to a request-response pair. The *APDU* request consists out of an obligatory header, containing the command and some further connection parameters (like the used channel). According to the command that is previously defined, a data body can be attached to the request. *APDU* responses then in turn possess the returned bits of information wrapped in a data body, as well as 2 byte trailer indicating either a successful or a failed communication.

3.3.2 Communication principle of Amiibos

Despite its rather easy usage, the *NFC* technology is with a maximum of $424kbit/s$ to $848kbit/s$ currently still limited to a field of applications with a rapid transfer of little data rates. Therefore, for the transmission of a large bulk of data it is considered good practice to use other signaling technologies instead. In this case *NFC* is only used in order to submit a special type of *NDEF Message* as the communication parameters that are required to establish the other connection. As the tag embedded in *Amiibos* only stores up to 540 byte, the communication is conveniently a direct peer-to-peer one and no further specialized connection handover is required.

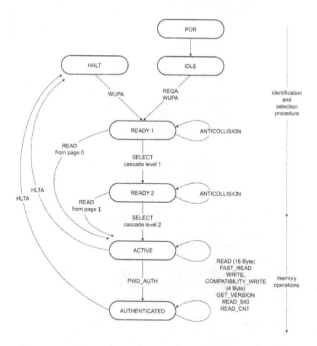

Figure 3.11: Communication principle of a *NTAG215 NFC* tag[28]

After the reading *NFC* unit initialized a magnetic field, every tag that comes within its range hence receives conducted electricity serving as a power source. This so-called **power-on reset** (marked as **POR** in figure 3.11 above) therefore switches the *NTAG215* to the **IDLE** state. The tag remains in this state for as long as the capacitive circuit is not broken off or until a **REQA** or **WUPA** request establishes the connection. The returned ATQA response then starts an anti-collision method in order to clearly distinguish the UID of the *NFC* tag the reader wants to communicate with. As the *Amiibos'* UIDs always possess a length of 7 byte, **SELECT** commands on two cascade levels are transmitted. For this, the first 0x9370 *SELECT* command returns a *SAK* response containing a cascade byte of 0x88, indicating that at least another cascade level exists, as well as the first three bytes of the UID. Furthermore, a bit count check byte, as the result of calculating an exclusive-or over the former four bytes, is returned. In case the check byte indicates a failed transaction, the same request is performed over and over again. Otherwise the second 0x9570 **SELECT** command is sent out. Hereby is another *SAK* response, with the last four bytes of the UID and another check byte set as content, obtained. The *NFC* tag will be set to an **ACTIVE** state, if this transmission does not fail. All operations that need no authentication can now be performed with the *data exchange protocol* request-response pairs. As for *Amiibos* the authentication process is only required in order to write data to the tag. All other commands can already become executed by now. This means that at this state the *Amiibo*'s data can be read (by the **READ** command) and that the version can be asked for (by **GET_VERSION**). Furthermore, it is even possible to request the signature (with passing on **READ_SIG**) as well as the internal *NFC* counter value (**READ_CNT**). By passing on the right password with the **PWD_AUTH** authentication command (0x1B & 4 hexadecimal password bytes), the tag is switched to the **AUTHENTICATED** state. Therefore, while being in this state, the data can be written back to the *NFC* tag with the **WRITE** command. If the password verification fails however, an internal counter for wrong attempts will be increased by one. Once this value becomes, without being reset by a valid registration, larger than a predefined maximum (for *Amiibos* this are seven tries) the tag will get inevitably locked and unable to either be read or written to. By the **HLTA** request is the tag deactivated again and does no longer respond to the reader. In order to re-establish the connection again, a **WUPA** command and the following **SELECT** cascade sequences need to be triggered.

3.4   Software project

The preceding sections and the bits of information regarding *Amiibos* within were the result of an autonomous research in this field. Therefore, these findings were also directly applied to the corresponding software project. As already mentioned in this chapter's header, an *Android* library for the basic *Amiibo* integration, as well as an *Android* application for the emulation of *Amiibos*, had been targeted at first. Due to several difficulties that however arose within the development phase, the scope of the software project was changed to the *Android* library in question and an *Android* application in order to backup *Amiibo* data. A screenshot taken from within the aforesaid app is displayed below in figure 3.12. The entire software solution had never been and will never be published for a usage outside of this bachelor thesis, as a lot of resources with a copyright by *Nintendo* were used.

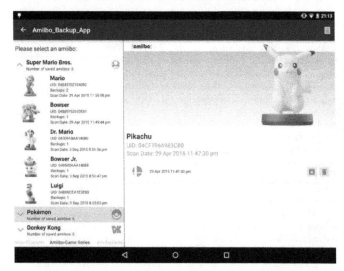

Figure 3.12: Screenshot taken from within the *Amiibo*-backup application (resources are attached in A.2) on a *HTC Nexus 9* running on *Android 5.1.1*

3.4.1   Emulating *Amiibos*

In order to completely emulate a *NFC* tag, it must operate in *card emulation mode*. To achieve this on *Android* devices, the feature of *Host-based Card Emulation* (*HCE*) is used[9]. Most of the time, a separate chip in the *NFC* enabled *Android* device (the so-called *Secure Element*) will emulate the tag.

For this, the tag to be emulated is first provisioned into the *Secure Element* by any application. Afterwards the device can route all data directly to this location. Since *Android KitKat* (version 4.4.*x*) a further method of *HCE* is available. This variant does not involve a *Secure Element* and hence instead of routing the protocol data units to the former, the data is passed on directly to the *host CPU*.

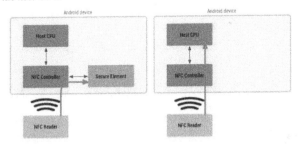

Figure 3.13: The functional principle of *Host-based Card Emulation* for *Android*: with a *Secure Element* (left) or without one (right)[9]

One essential requirement for the utilization of *Host-based Card Emulation* on an *Android* device is, that the tag to emulate is based on several *ISO/IEC 7816* standards and hence uses an *APDU* structure. As the *NTAG215 NFC* tag within an *Amiibo* is however based on the *ISO/IEC 14443-2 Type A* definition, *HCE* thus cannot be used to emulate *Amiibos*. If not a stock *Android* image, but rather *CyanogenMod* version 9 or above, is used as the device's operating system, this restriction does not exist any longer. But still, this does not change the fact that *ISO/IEC 14443-2* based tags cannot be emulated either. Some devices then in turn possess a special embedded *NFC* controller (like the *LG Nexus 5*) that would also allow the emulation of this tag type. But this functionality is not yet implemented, as the possible gain of this would be generally speaking near nominal, compared to the enormous effort of implementing this feature. Therefore, updating the for this purpose required native libraries and rebuilding a custom image of *CyanogenMod* or *Android* would clearly exceed the scope of the software project for the bachelor thesis. Hence the software project was changed to an application in order to backup *Amiibo* data.

3.4.2 Backing up *Amiibos*

In order to use an *Android* device for the communication with a *NFC* tag, several precautions have to be made. This means that especially within the *AndroidManifest.xml* file of the *Android* project several xml-tags have to be defined first.

As *NFC* is only supported since *Android Gingerbread* (version 2.3.3) this has to be remarked in the code with:

```
<!-- Android 2.3.3+ (API level 10) is at least required -->
<uses-sdk android:minSdkVersion='10' android:
    targetSdkVersion='23'/>
```

Furthermore, in order to grant the access permission to the *NFC* feature and to limit the application to *NFC* enabled devices, the following lines of code are used:

```
<!-- Request permission to use NFC -->
<!-- Note that by targeting Android Marshmallow (6.0.x; API
    level 23) permissions are handled at runtime! -->
<uses-permission android:name='android.permision.NFC'/>

<!-- Restrict the usage to NFC enabled devices -->
<uses-feature android:name='android.hardware.nfc' android:
    required='true'/>
```

3.4.2.1 Establishing a connection

At this point all precautions are made and a connection can be established at any time. For this, an *Android Activity* starts receiving *Intents* whenever a *NFC* tag comes within reach. In order to avoid wild cards (because we would like to limit the interactions to *Amiibo* tags though) an *Intent*-filter needs to be set. *Amiibos* are based upon the *NFC Type A* signaling technology, whereas this needs to be defined within an xml-file as a tech-list:

```
<!-- Amiibo tags fall within these 3 definitions, hence
    filter for these Intent-flags -->
<tech-list>
    <tech>android.nfc.tech.NfcA</tech>
    <tech>android.nfc.tech.MifareClassic</tech>
    <tech>android.nfc.tech.MifareUltralight</tech>
</tech-list>
```

At last this *Intent*-filter needs to be mapped in the *AndroidManifest.xml* to the *Activity* that should respond to the *Amiibos*. Therefore, the following code snippet is put within the corresponding *Activity*'s root tag:

```
<intent-filter>
    <action android:name="android.nfc.action.TECH_DISCOVERED"/>
    <category android:name="android.intent.category.DEFAULT"/>
</intent-filter>
<!-- The resource marks the former defined tech-list -->
<meta-data android:name="android.nfc.action.TECH_DISCOVERED"
    android:resource="@xml/nfc_tech_filter"/>
```

By now the *Activity* only receives *Intents* from tags within range that have the same properties as *Amiibos*. Stored within these *Intents* are objects that represent the state of the found *NFC* tag at the time of its discovery. Therefore, these representations can be obtained in the *Activity*'s overridden onNewIntent(Intent) method by:

```
@Override
protected void onNewIntent(Intent intent){
    //Important to call the super method here too
    super.onNewIntent(intent);

    //Just to be sure if this Intent was the one received from the Amiibo
    if(NfcAdapter.ACTION_TECH_DISCOVERED.equals(intent.getAction())){
        //The Intent came from the Amiibo, now get the tag reference
        Tag nfcTag = intent.getParcelableExtra(NfcAdapter.EXTRA_TAG);
        //Better 'cast' it to a MifareUltralight, to use a high-level API later
        MifareUltralight amiiboTag = MifareUltralight.get(nfcTag);
    }
}
```

3.4.2.2 Reading the *Amiibo* s data

Once we received the *MifareUltralight* object, the tag's data can be read. For this, the amiiboTag.connect() method needs to get executed first in order to connect to the *NFC* tag. Afterwards exactly 16 byte can be read at once by each amiiboTag.readPages(pageIndex) call. After all the desired data had been read, the amiiboTag.close() method needs to get called in order to close the connection again, as this allows the connection with other tag objects.

Algorithm 3.3: Reading *Amiibo* data

INPUT: The *Amiibo* tag reference as *MifareUltralight* object
OUTPUT: 135 pages (540 byte) stored on the *Amiibo*

1: **try**
2:      Connect to *Amiibo*
3:      **for** ($i = 0$ to $\frac{134}{4}$) **do**   . 4 pages (32 bit) are read at once
4:          Read 4 pages beginning at index $4 * i$
5:          Save the received values
6:      **end for**
7:      Close connection to *Amiibo*
8:      Return the saved data read from the *Amiibo*
9: **catch** (No connection to tag.)

3.4.2.3 Writing data to the *Amiibo*

In strong comparison to the reading procedure, the *Amiibo* needs to get authenticated before data can be written back to the tag. Therefore, right after the obligatory amiiboTag.connect(), an amiiboTag.tranceive() procedure, with the $0x1B$ PWD_AUTH command byte and the 32-bit password as parameters, needs to get executed. Only in case this transaction succeeded, an amiiboTag.writePage(pageIndex, 32-bit proprietary data) can be used to write the data back again.

Algorithm 3.4: Writing data to the *Amiibo*

INPUT: The *Amiibo* tag reference as *MifareUltralight* object
1: **try**
2:    Connect to *Amiibo*
3:    Execute authentication command   . requires the 32-bit password
4:    **for** ($i = 0$ to 134) **do**
5:        **if** (The page address i is not locked) **then**
6:            Write 4-byte array to page address i
7:        **else**
8:            Do not try to write the data to the page address i
9:        **end if**
10:    **end for**
11:    Close connection to *Amiibo*
12: **catch** (No connection to tag./Authentication failed.)

The aforesaid *Android* library for basic *Amiibo* integration therefore eases the usage as it already implements these features. Furthermore, the read data would only be available in its byte-wise representation, whereas the library automatically parses it into a human readable form on the principle of the *Amiibo* data page table as well. For example, this means that *Amiibos* are right after being scanned also recognized by their appropriate *Amiibo* series, their type and the video game character they represent. Additionally several more functions for an easier interaction with *Amiibos* are provided in the library too, like getting the UID or comparing the *NFC* counter value.

As the *Android* application uses this library, it is hence also possible to scan *Amiibos*, to stack all their different save states within and, in case the password would be available, to write the data back to a certain *Amiibo*. Based on the latest standards of the *Android Material Design*, the user interface visually displays the gathered list of all scanned *Amiibos*. For this, it is also possible to further sort the list by four predefined criteria: video game characters, video game series, *Amiibo* series & *Amiibo* types.

Chapter 4

Conclusion

4.1 Conclusion

Near field communication based platforms in gaming are basically just *NFC* tags that are nicely wrapped by some sort of plastic toy, depicting a well-known video game character. Consequently they form a phygital (physical and digital) extension to the video games that implement a support for them. Hence depending on the video game and the figure, the figurine has a specialized purpose. On the one hand new content can be unlocked within the game, but on the other hand even some more complex interactions can be possible. Also special about this technology is that the save data from within the game is not stored on the gaming console, but rather on the tag per se. At the time of writing, three big franchises (namely *Skylanders, Disney Infinity* & *Amiibo*) and one (*Lego Dimensions*) that is shortly released after the submission of this bachelor thesis, exist within this field. Especially the technology of *Amiibos* had been highlighted, as the corresponding software project is also based on it. Based on these findings, an *Android* library for a basic *Amiibo* integration as well as an *Android* application for backing up *Amiibo* data was implemented. Despite a *NFC Forum Type 2* tag is embedded, a special data page table representation is used for *Amiibos* and not all standards are therefore met. *Elliptic curve cryptography* is used for the tag's digital signature, as well as for the generation of a 32-bit password for the overall security of *Amiibos*.

4.2 Future of *NFC* in gaming

As *Disney* acquired *Lucasfilm* back in 2012, the company also gained the rights to the *Star Wars* franchise as a result. For *Disney Infinity 3.0: Play Without Limits* that is scheduled to be released in autumn 2015 one of the many upcoming figure sets is based upon *Star Wars* characters and is therefore already going to be distributed at launch. All previously released

Disney Infinity NFC figurines from the two former editions will still be compatible with version 3.0. The following chart 4.1 hence visually displays the course of the evolution of this technology and indicates the amount of available figure models at specific dates.

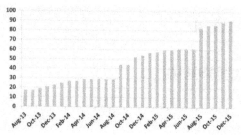

Figure 4.1: Chart displaying the amount of released *Disney Infinity* figurines over the time

Then again, especially September 2015 is going to play an important role for the future of *NFC* based platforms in gaming, with the release of both *Lego Dimensions* and *Skylanders: Super Charger*. At the initial release of *Lego Dimensions* already 14 different sets, which all are based on different franchises, will be available. This number is going to be constantly increased over the time, as by now it is confirmed that at least six new franchises will get included post launch.

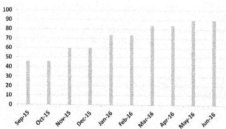

Figure 4.2: Chart displaying the plans for of releasing *Lego Dimensions* figurines over the time

The product line of *Skylanders: Super Charger* is already the fifth installment of this series, whereas a total amount of 372 different figures exists even before its market entrance. Furthermore, the first *Amiibo-Skylander* crossover figurines are going to be part of this line-up. *Activision* also announced that in 2016 battle cards, similar to the *Amiibo* cards, starring *Skylanders* and their enemies will be launched. The corresponding video gaming software however is in turn not bound to any gaming console, but rather it is only deployed on *iOS* and *Android* devices. Just like for the other entries of this series, right after being scanned the *Skylanders* will be transferred for their usage into the game.

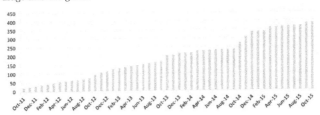

Figure 4.3: Chart displaying the amount of released *Skylanders* figurines over the time

Then again *Amiibos* possess an extremely big and dedicated fan base, as the announcement of every figure is being eagerly awaited. This is one of the reasons why most of the figurine contingents are already out of stock shortly after the initial launch. Sometimes *Nintendo* is still not even capable of providing additional delivery units due to the tremendous demand. Therefore, some character models are really seldom and are thus occasionally sold for up to four or five times the original price. Sometimes even defect *Amiibos* with a production fault that makes them unique in a special way are sold at high prices. For example a *Samus Aran Amiibo* which featured two arm canons instead of just one had been sold for approximately $2.500. An even more staggering price of $25.100 (by a normal price of $13/€15) was paid for a *Princess Peach Amiibo* that had no legs and hence seemed to float in the air. Then again the multi-platform video game *Shovel Knight* will get its own *Amiibo* in October 2015 and therefore also possibly smooths the way for further third-party *Amiibos*.

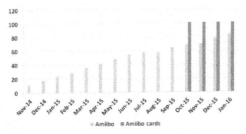

Figure 4.4: Chart displaying the amount of released *Amiibo* figurines over the time

All in all, the future of *NFC* based platforms in gaming looks rather bright, as the market for this segment is constantly growing. For this, the companies are frequently updating their product assortment and hence new figures are launched every month. Furthermore, long-term plans exist in order to keep the brands exciting and attractive to the gamers. Thus many presentations at the latest installment of the *Electronic Entertainment Expo* in 2015 were heavily influenced by the "toy to life"-concept, mostly in order to show off these plans to the public. Altogether it can be stated that the demand for new figures of all the existing franchises in this market segment will not cease any time soon. Even though the functionality within video games might not always properly adapt to the increasing assortment, the "toy to life"-figures are nevertheless still commonly used as collectible items. With all of this in mind, I am very sure this *NFC* technology in gaming will accompany us gaming enthusiasts for a very long time.

Appendix A

Please take note that the CD-Rom is not part of this publication.

Content of the CD-ROM

Format: CD-ROM, Single Layer, ISO9660-Format

A.1 Bachelor thesis

Pfad: /

    petereder_nfc_based_platforms_in_gaming.pdf Bachelor thesis *Near field communication based platforms in gaming* as a PDF-file

    Latex_Files/ . . . . . . LaTeX-files

A.2 Project les

Pfad: Project/

    Amiibo_Library/ . . . . Source-folder of an *Android*-based library for basic *Amiibo* integration

    Amiibo_Backup_App/ Source-folder of an *Android* application used for *Amiibo* Backups

    Sources_Support_Library/ Source-folder of the *Android-Support v7 Appcompat library* (Revision 22) with customized changes

    Sources_Custom_Support_Library_v4/ Source-folder of the *Android-Support v4 library* (Revision 22) with customized source code

A.3 Amiibo les

Pfad: Amiibo_Files/

Amiibo_Dumps/ . . . .   Folder containing gathered dumped *Amiibo* tags

Amiibo_Sni er_Traces/   Folder containing gathered *Amiibo* traces with a *NFC* Sniffer

A.4   Literature

Pfad: Literature/

NFC_roland_langer.pdf   Literature [24]

NFC_cuno.pdf . . . . .   Literature [14]

RFID_overview.pdf . .   Literature [32]

NTAG213_215_216.pdf   Literature [28]

NFC_Technology_Games.pdf   Literature [33]

Skylanders_NFC_in_livingroom.pdf   Literature [13]

ESA-Essential-Facts-2015.pdf   Literature [10]

NFC_Gami cation.pdf   Literature [21]

NFC_toys_educational.pdf   Literature [11]

NFC_augmented_toy_environment.pdf   Literature [23]

Gami cation_in_Softwareentwicklung.pdf   Literature [16]

NFC_AR_Interaction_MGaming.pdf   Literature [15]

NFC_ubiquitous_games.pdf   Literature [17]

hinske_classifyingpervasivegames.pdf   Literature [19]

NFC_Forum_Type_Tags.pdf   Literature [27]

NFCForum_Type-2-Tag.pdf   Literature [26]

GuideEllipticCurveCryptography.pdf   Literature [18]

koppensteiner_diplomarbeit.pdf   Literature [20]

ellipticCurves_cryptography_elaine.pdf   Literature [12]

Understanding_Cryptography   Literature [29]

ecc_encryption . . . . .   Literature [22]

ECC_Standards_v1.0 .   Literature [31]

A.5   Online sources

Pfad: Online_Sources/

nfc_forum_org_speci cations_and_application.pdf   Literature [3]

nfc_forum_org_what_is_nfc_what_it_does.pdf   Literature [2]

www_gameswelt_at_special_sinn_und_unsinn_von_amiibo.pdf
Literature [4]

www_near eldcommunication_org_nfc_signaling.pdf Literature [1]
www_safaribooksonline_com_ndef.pdf Literature [5]
arstechnica_primer_ecc.pdf Literature [6]
NFC_basics_android_developer.pdf Literature [7]
NFC_advanced_android_developer.pdf Literature [8]
NFC_HCE_android_developer.pdf Literature [9]

A.6   Images

Pfad: Images/

BA-images/ . . . . folder containing all images used in this bachelor thesis

Project-screenshots/ . . folder containing screenshots taken from within the software project's *Android* application

References

Literature

[10] Entertainment Software Association. *2015 Sales, demographic and usage data. Essential facts about the computer and vide game industry.* statistics. USA: Entertainment Software Association, 2015 (cit. on pp. 1, 53).

[11] Emilia Biffi et al. "NFC-based application with educational purposes". In: *8th International Conference on Pervasive Computing Technologies for Healthcare.* (May 20 23, 2014). Oldenburg, Germany, 2014, pp. 370 372 (cit. on p. 53).

[12] Elaine Brow. "Elliptic Curve Cryptography". 2010 (cit. on p. 53).

[13] Paul Coulton. "SKYLANDERS: Near Field in Your Living Room Now". In: *Ubiquity: The Journal of Pervasive Media* 1 (September/October 2012), pp. 136 138 (cit. on pp. 3, 53).

[14] Andrea Cuno. "Near field Communication". German. Munich, Germany: Technische Universitt Mnchen, 2010 (cit. on pp. 9, 15, 53).

[15] Erik Einebrant. "NFC and AR Interaction in Mobile Gaming". Gothenburg, Sweden: Chalmers University of Technology, 2012 (cit. on pp. 2, 53).

[16] Michael Fecher. "Gamification in der Softwareentwicklung: Chancen und Mglichkeiten". German. Wrzburg-Schweinfurt, Germany: Hochschule fr angewandte Wissenschaften Wrzburg-Schweinfurt, 2012 (cit. on p. 53).

[17] Pilar Castro Garrido et al. "Near Field Communication in the Development of Ubiquitous Games". Crdoba, Spain: University of Crdoba, 2010 (cit. on p. 53).

[18] Darrel Hankerson, Alfred Menezes, and Scott Vanstone. *Guide to Elliptic Curve Cryptography.* Springer, 2004 (cit. on pp. 34, 53).

[19] Steve Hinske et al. "Classifying Pervasive Games: On Pervasive Computing and Mixed Reality". Zurich, Switzerland: Institute for Pervasive Computing (cit. on pp. 2, 53).

[20] Clemens Koppensteiner. "Mathematical Foundations of Elliptic Curve Cryptography". Vienna University of Technology, 2009 (cit. on p. 53).

[21] Matthias Kranz, Lukas Murmann, and Florian Michahelles. "Research in the Large: Challenges for Large-Scale Mobile Application Research. A Case Study about NFC Adoption using Gamification via an App Store". 2013 (cit. on p. 53).

[22] D. Sravana Kumar, CH. Suneetha, and A. Chandrasekh. "Encryption of data using Elliptic Curve over finite fields". In: *International Journal of Distributed and Parallel S ystems* 3 (January 2012), pp. 301 308 (cit. on p. 53).

[23] Matthias Lampe, Steve Hinske, and Sandra Brockmann. "Mobile Device-based Interaction Patterns in Augmented Toy Environments". Zurich, Switzerland: Institute for Pervasive Computing, 2006 (cit. on p. 53).

[24] Josef Langer and Michael Roland. *Anwendungen und Technik von Near Field Communication (NFC)*. German. Hagenberg, Austria: Springer-Verlag Berlin Heidelberg, Mar. 2010 (cit. on pp. 9 12, 14, 16, 17, 19, 22, 37, 38, 53).

[25] *NFC Forum NFC Data Exchange Format (NDEF)*. Technical Specification. Version 1.0. NFC Forum. July 2006.

[26] *NFC Forum Type 2 Tag Operation Specification*. Technical Specification. Version 1.1. NFC Forum. May 2011 (cit. on pp. 20 22, 53).

[27] *NFC Forum Type Tags. White Paper V1.0*. Technical Specification. Version 1.0. NXP Semiconductors. Apr. 2009 (cit. on p. 53).

[28] *NTAG213/215/216. NFC Forum Type 2 Tag compliant IC with 144/504/888 bytes user memory*. Product data sheet. Version 3.1. NXP Semiconductors. Dec. 2013 (cit. on pp. 20, 21, 24, 25, 41, 53).

[29] Christof Paar and Jan Pelzl. *Understanding Cryptography. A Textbook for Students and Practitioners*. Springer, 2009 (cit. on pp. 30 32, 34, 53).

[30] Dominique Paret, Xavier Boutonnier, and Youssef Houiti. *NFC (Near Field Communication). Principes et applications de la communication en champ proche*. French. Dunod, 2012 (cit. on p. 22).

[31] *STANDARDS FOR EFFICIENT CRYPTOGRAPHY. SEC2: Recommended Elliptic Curve Domain Parameters*. Standard reference. Version 1.0. Certicom Research. Sept. 2010 (cit. on pp. 36, 53).

[32] Ron Weinstein. "RFID: A Technical Overview and Its Application to the Enterprise". In: *IT Professional* 7 (May/June 2005), pp. 27 33 (cit. on pp. 10, 53).

[33] Jennifer Zaino. "NFC Technology brings new life to games". In: *RFID Journal* 9 (September/October 2012), pp. 28 32 (cit. on p. 53).

Online sources

[1] URL: http://www.near eldcommunication.org/nfc-signaling.html (visited on 05/25/2015) (cit. on pp. 14, 54).

[2] URL: http://nfc-forum.org/what-is-nfc/what-it-does/ (visited on 05/30/2015) (cit. on pp. 15, 53).

[3] URL: http://nfc-forum.org/our-work/speci cations-and-application-documents/speci cations/protocol-technical-speci cations/ (visited on 05/31/2015) (cit. on p. 53).

[4] URL: http://www.gameswelt.at/wii-u/special/sinn-und-unsinn-von-amiibo- guren,238143 (visited on 05/25/2015) (cit. on p. 53).

[5] URL: https://www.safaribooksonline.com/library/view/beginning-nfc/9781449324094/ch04.html (visited on 05/31/2015) (cit. on pp. 16, 54).

[6] URL: http://arstechnica.com/security/2013/10/a-relatively-easy-to-understand-primer-on-elliptic-curve-cryptography/ (visited on 07/14/2015) (cit. on pp. 32, 33, 54).

[7] URL: https://developer.android.com/guide/topics/connectivity/nfc/nfc.html (visited on 08/22/2015) (cit. on p. 54).

[8] URL: https://developer.android.com/guide/topics/connectivity/nfc/advanced-nfc.html (visited on 08/22/2015) (cit. on p. 54).

[9] URL: https://developer.android.com/guide/topics/connectivity/nfc/hce.html (visited on 08/22/2015) (cit. on pp. 43, 44, 54).